J. Gordon Kingsley

What Can We Really Believe?

12 Sermons That Make Sense

Beloit, Wisconsin
Turtle Creek Publications
2015

—

Turtle Creek Publications
2067 W. Collingswood Drive
Beloit, WI 53511
gordon.kingsley3@gmail.com

ISBN-13: 978-0692415238

To the Memory of My Father,
Rev. J. Gordon Kingsley, Sr.,
who would have approved of scarcely a word
in the theology of these sermons,
though his spirit would secretly have applauded
my efforts at practical common sense.
And, most important,
who would have smiled his warm smile,
maybe chuckled a time or two at the ironies,
and loved me
"Anyhow."

Contents

Preface and Acknowledgments

I preached my first sermon at Calvary Baptist Church in Columbia, MO in 1951. Not sure of the date, though I could probably find not only the date but the sermon itself in an old box somewhere if I would seriously rummage and dig in life's leavings. I do remember the title: "Break Down the Idols." I think the text was from II Chronicles 34, and it was about the young King Josiah who at age fifteen was breaking down pagan idols during one of those periodic cleansings of Judah and Jerusalem that punctuated this period of what we call Old Testament history.

I was probably feeling some identification with the young king, for I was a "hot gospeller wannabe" at seventeen years old, still a senior at David Henry Hickman High School. We used to have a name for what I was then, as a class—we were called, and even called ourselves, "preacher boys." There were quite a few of us in Calvary Baptist at that time. My dad was our pastor. (When your dad is your preacher, it's a trip; when your preacher is your dad, it's an even bigger trip!) He was very effective in "youth work," as well as in building up congregations and raising church edifices, and in the waves of revivalism that characterized our Calvary communion in those days quite a few of us "heard the call" and "surrendered to preach." It is both a strength and a weakness of Baptists that they encourage their young "preacher boys" to get into the pulpit early, and thus it was that at so tender an age I was standing in the pulpit at Calvary, peering out into the congregation through my always-crooked glasses, and stumbling through an exercise in chastising and redeeming my elders.

It was the beginning of what became the "spine," the core of my life's work, though I didn't always recognize it all the time. For my calling led me not into the pastorate, but into a life in university education, health care, and briefly in a great art museum. (Mom thought I had "left the ministry" and wasn't happy about it, though she never flagged in her love toward and pride in her children.) Always, though, whatever the job description, there was the preaching: in small rural churches, in large city churches, in colleges and universities, in religious conventions, and in both America and Britain.

And, truth be told, though I probably would not have recognized the fact and may have even denied it, I was "preaching" a lot of times, in a "secular" sense and in "secular" contexts, when leading colleges or serving in health care or taking responsibilities in civic life. It was called "being a speaker," and it occurred in civic gatherings and university auditoriums, at dinners and conventions and professional meetings, ultimately all across America and a bit— though with lesser scope—in the English Midlands as well. "Speaking" became a major vehicle, an important implement, in what leading and serving I was privileged to do.

Why am I saying all this in a Preface to a volume of sermons? I think to explain that, often unconsciously, I never stopped being a preacher, whatever else was going on. As a college president of a church-related school I preached throughout our domain of influence as a means of outreach for our college—though I was always scrupulous about leading *worship*, not indulging in *promotion*. Meanwhile, the "secular preaching" was going on in the civic arena, and this continued when I became a vice president of the huge Health Midwest organization, one of two major health systems in Kansas City and its region.

Thus it was that in the last year of my tenure with Health Midwest, before I shipped out in January 2003 to be Principal of Harlaxton College in England, I was honored by the invitation to serve as "Interim Senior Minister" at the great Country Club Christian Church in Kansas City. It was at that time—and still is, I gather--the great mainline "preaching church" of that part of the United States and a congregation of considerable community influence—being located in such a "posh" part of the city and so attractive to a professional clientele that I couldn't resist telling them I was a "missionary to the up and outs."

Country Club Christian (named for a residential district in Kansas City and not, as the bad joke went, a religious clubhouse at the first tee) was a thoughtful, open, supportive congregation. In theology it was about as far from the fundamentalist Calvary Baptist of my youth as a church could get. By the time I joined them as their minister, I was no longer responsible for the wellbeing of a Baptist college, therefore no longer vulnerable to the slings and arrows of some of the excessively conservative and excessively opinionated Baptist brethren. And so, for the first time in my life I was totally free to think through what really made sense to me as a Christian, to formulate those thoughts in sermons for fellow seekers, and to share in a Christian community of intellectual depth and spiritual challenge, of open spirits and caring hearts. They weren't patsies at CCCC: they would listen carefully — well, some of them would — and challenge what I said to them. And that was good, too.

So that's how these sermons came about, in 2002 — a half century after that first hot gospelling sermon at Calvary Baptist Church in Columbia.

These twelve sermons are themselves just a portion of those offered during that year of preaching, of course, but in them I deliberately addressed (pondered over, did my best to make sense of) the classic doctrinal areas of Christian theology: Religious Authority, the Nature of God (Immanence and Transcendence), the Person of Jesus Christ (Christology), the Holy Spirit (Pneumatology), Salvation (Soteriology), the Problem of Evil (Theodicy), the Nature of Humankind (Anthropology), "Last Things" (Eschatology), the Church (Ecclesiology), and how our Beliefs shape our Walk with God (Make-It-Real-and-Get-It-Done-ology).

I know it all sounds pretty heavy. But what I have sought to do (as neither a proper scholar nor a theologian, though reasonably literate and occasionally even thoughtful) is to consider these classic doctrines from the viewpoint of the person in the pew — "What do all these big theological words mean, anyway, and what difference do they make in my life?" Theology in isolation is useless: it has to "come alive" in the days and ways of real people living real lives.

My earnest desire, then, has been to "make these things make sense" in our everyday living. Hence the title, *What Can We Really Believe? 12 Sermons that Make Sense*. It is all an effort at a *Theology in a Practical Key*, and you as reader will have to determine how successful it is in your own thinking — and more important, in your own living.

There is a gap of years between the preaching of these sermons in 2002 and the publishing in 2015 — I plead guilty to leading a college on foreign soil during those years and from happy necessity focusing on those tasks instead of revisiting and revising sermons. That gap dictated that now, from the vantage point of today, I revise and update some of the matter, though not so much as to obliterate the place and context that gave birth to these messages. These were real messages to real people at a real place and time, and I want that immediacy to come through.

For example, these sermons were offered during the year just after, some of them just at the first anniversary of, the terrorist attack on the World Trade Towers in New York; and so that event reverberates a bit through the pages. I updated and expanded some of the references to 9-1-1, but mostly I let them be: that event was such a major scarring evil in American history, and most certainly in recent American experience, that its voice should still be heard.

But mostly, you will find that the content relates not to external history but to our personal histories, our own understanding of God and our own walk with God. And that's the point.

Some words of acknowledgment, in genuine thanks:

To Richard W. Brown, then my boss as CEO of Health Midwest and now CEO of American Century Funds and the Stowers Institute, who not only permitted but encouraged my taking the Interim Senior Minister Role at Country Club Christian in addition to my "day job" for that great hospital and health care organization.

To the congregation of Country Club Christian Church, who invited me to come and minister among them, who taught me, who loved me, and who sent me off to serve in England a better person than when they found me on their doorstep (side door, not front).

To generations of good people, "saints of God," whom I have followed or led, or followed and led and the same time, during a lifetime in the church: teachers, pastors, friends, family.

To my father, to whom this book is dedicated, for instilling in me not just a head belief that our faith matters, but a sense of it deep in my marrowbones, way past just "thinking" or "believing," but more like what the Proto-Indo-European language calls *kred-dhel*, "heart put/place" — a "creed" [*kred*] that becomes a part of who we are. Dad was, as I am, as each of us is, a deeply flawed person, all the while being a fundamentally good and loving man. And I probably "caught" my *kred-dhel* from him more than I was "taught" it by him and Mom and many others.

To Robert Soileau, also, like my father, "of blessed memory," a passionate professor of theology and a decent, thoroughly honest man, who first began to open the stuck-shut eyelids of my mind and heart through his brilliant seminary lectures in theology and continued this gift of grace through his friendship until the day he died. To me, he was the epitome of the "great" professor.

To two particular friends from seminary days and since, Walter Byron Shurden and William Powell Tuck, both of them outstanding preachers and writers and church leaders. Who would have thought it in those early-morning discussions on Gentilly Boulevard/Chef Menteur Highway as we did battle with the writing of our seminar papers, all the while keeping ourselves awake by gulping gallons of theological coffee, dark New Orleans coffee 'n chicory, thick as river mud and tangy as original sin. They were great friends; they became great men and servants of God, and it didn't even ruin them.

Dag Hammarskjöld wrote the words: "To all that has been, I say 'Thanks.' To all that will be, I say 'Yes.'"

Gordon Kingsley
Easter, 2015

"Just Tell Me What To Believe, and I'll Believe It."

"What Can We Really Believe?"
Theology in a Practical Key: Understanding Religious Authority

Deuteronomy 26:5-9.   Deuteronomy 26:8-9: "The Lord brought us out of Egypt with a mighty hand and an outstretched arm, with a terrifying display of power, and with signs and wonders, and he brought us into this place and gave us this land, a land flowing with milk and honey."

Bill Bell said it to me, in New Orleans.

Bill worked for Upton Press, a good printing firm in town. He had married the boss's daughter, which, along with his own considerable talents, had made him a vice president and put him in line to take over the company. He planned, as he said, to make a lot of money fast, invest it well, retire young, and then "get me a tweed jacket with leather patches on the elbows, and a pipe to puff, and go teach in a college."

Somehow he had decided that I might be working in a college or university at his retirement day, and he asked me to remember him and hire him when he was ready. I explained that if I were in a college it might well be church related, and there would no doubt be some expectations of Christian belief for faculty members. This fazed Bill not at all: "No problem," said he. "You just tell me what to believe, and I'll believe it."

"You tell me what to believe, and I'll believe it."

How often we feel this way. Sometimes out of spiritual laziness or fuzziness or carelessness. We just don't want to be bothered about thinking it all through, or reading it through, or praying it through. So, just as a matter of ease and convenience, if we can get someone to tell us what to believe, we'll believe it.

Or sometimes it is out of plain old confusion.   There are so many religions, so many people claiming to be right, so many doctrines and

---

1

dogmas and rules that we don't really know what to think. It would be so comforting to say, "Just tell me what to believe, and I'll believe it."

All of us, at one time or another, yearn for a billboard or bumper sticker kind of religion, with clear, easy teachings we can "buy." We would like a short list of beliefs — not more than one page, or a handy-dandy handbook. Keep it simple, keep it brief, make it real, and if possible make it painless. "Just tell me what to believe, and I'll believe it."

Oh, I do wish it were all so easy. I wish all choices were clear, all decisions simple, all demands uncomplicated, all actions straightforward. That is the strong, enduring appeal of any kind of strongly-stated dogma, any fundamentalism, whether it is religious or political or social or educational.

It offers answers.
Those answers are simple, clear, direct, and emotionally powerful.
Those answers claim to be exclusively true.
And those answers offer the sense of security that "truth" can bring.

Unfortunately, those answers are also wrong. Or at least not completely right.

For life is not simple, and easy answers do not fit the complex real life situations in which we find ourselves. When I was a young professor, before I had a clue what I meant by what I was doing, I hung on the wall of my tiny teacher-y office a little plaque which read, "There is a simple answer to every question: Neat. Plausible. And Wrong."

So "what's a mother to do?" asked the old commercial. "What's a serious person to do?" we ask.

Hearing dozens of voices, all claiming to be right, all asking our commitment and loyalty, all promising security and salvation and freedom, what *do* we believe? How *do* we behave? How *do* we establish that daily, living relationship with a loving God that is the goal, the end of all our belief and behavior, all our theology and our morality?

We are asking, here, the question of religious knowledge and, behind that, the question of religious authority. It is the first, most basic question in any theology, and so we consider it first in this sermon series on *What Can We Really Believe? Theology in a Practical Key.* How can I know God? How can I know what is right? How can I know what I should do? What source (or sources) gives me those answers?

And the even larger question is this: how can I have *real* answers, *clear* answers on the one hand while avoiding extremism or fanaticism on the other. How can I stand for something, be a person of conviction, yet be open to new truth and to others who hold different views? These are our questions for this morning.

And let's start inside your own head. Where *do* your beliefs come from? When you think about it, you will probably give several sources: From teachings in your family, the way you were brought up. From your church. From the Bible, no doubt. From your reasoning, your thinking things out. From your feelings, your intuitions. From your experience. And you stir all that up into a thick, rich spiritual stew, one which nourishes soul and life.

The problem is that it *is* a stew, a combination of many things, when what we want is something simple and straightforward — good old doctrinal fried chicken, maybe, or — more likely — a delicious spiritual lollipop. Or back to an earlier metaphor: we get a dissertation when what we want is a bumper sticker, one we can slap on the rear end of our souls that says something simple, anything simple, that will "just tell us what to believe, and we'll believe it."

For example, lots of people, particularly Catholic people, wear a bumper sticker that says, LISTEN TO THE CHURCH. This is very, very good advice, for the church has taught us and nourished us from our youth; or, beginning now, it can teach us and nourish us and bring us truth. The church gave us the Bible, historians say. The church offers a supporting fellowship, provides a kind of discipline, gives a place of worship, organizes opportunities to serve, becomes a voice for good in the community, teaches us, inspires us, gives us a structure for our faith. The church also connects us with believers around the world, makes us part of a movement that is thousands of years old, that has shaped our society and even our civilization for good. LISTEN TO THE CHURCH, is bumper sticker #1.

And that would be enough for any of us if there weren't so many different kinds of churches, or if they all agreed, or if they weren't sometimes subject to the errors of us imperfect mortals who are their members. But they don't always agree! In the Eucharist, for example, does the bread and wine actually *become* in its substance, its essence, the body and blood of our Lord, or does it *symbolize* his body and blood? Doctrines of different churches will vary on this point, and it is critically important to some. Should we be filled with the Holy Ghost, speak in tongues? Or at an Appalachian extreme, should we handle snakes as part of our worship, because the Gospels of Mark and Luke predict it might be done with impunity and St. Paul on the Island of Malta is described as doing so, as recorded in Acts 28?

My former colleague Glen Stassen told of one of his classes at Duke Divinity School in which a guest lecturer from England was arguing vigorously for total freedom in all matters of worship when a student interrupted to ask if such freedom extended even to the handling of poisonous snakes, as some mountain worshippers did and still do. The Englishman was going so fast he scarcely heard the question and was just in process of repeating, "Yes, Yes, any religious expression is legitimate," when the student's question registered in his head and he stopped short: "Snaiks, you saiy?" Snakes were just a bit too much, even for an impassioned, freedom-loving Brit!

LISTEN TO THE CHURCH, reads this good bumper sticker. But the listening must be done with discrimination, mustn't it, whatever our religious brand name, understanding always that our points of agreement across Christendom are much larger and more important than our points of disagreement. Unfortunately, we fuss and fight and feud over the differences, way too much, like little brothers slapping each other around. LISTEN TO THE CHURCH. It is one way to truth.

Other persons, mainly Protestant, will affix a bumper sticker which reads, JUST BELIEVE THE BIBLE. We sang about it as children, in Sunday school or Vacation Bible School:

> The B-I-B-L-E,
> Yes that's the Book for me.
> I stand alone on the word of God,
> The B-I-B-L-E!

My fundamentalist minister father would say it over and over, in private sermons to me as his son as well as in public sermons to his congregations: "God said it. I believe it. That settles it." He was speaking of the Bible. The great German Reformer Martin Luther, a priest and monk seeking to cure serious excesses in the church of his time, turned to *sola scriptura, sola fide* — "scripture alone, faith alone" — as the basis of his Ninety-Five Theses nailed to the church door in Wittenberg on All Saints Eve, 1517. Thomas Campbell, in the earliest days of the Christian Church/Disciples of Christ movement, on August 17, 1809, in a meeting at the home of Abraham Alters in Washington, PA, expressed the core belief of what would be a new church in the slogan, "Where the scriptures speak, we speak; where the scriptures are silent, we are silent."

As Protestants, we revere the Bible, we honor the Bible, we defend the Bible, some of us would die for the Bible. We also don't read it very much.

Yet our bumper sticker, JUST BELIEVE THE BIBLE, is a good one. The Bible, an inspired collection of books, shows us how others walked the walk of faith for centuries, gives us teachings that help us understand God and Jesus, offers compelling evidence of God's love toward us and our duty to act in love toward others, details the foundations for all Christian theology, tells us how to live our lives in a vital walk with God right now, in our day.

The Bible is a difficult book in that it comes from cultures entirely different from ours. The Old Testament, for example, accepts multiple wives and even handmaidens — we don't read much of handymen in those patriarchal documents. The New Testament accepts slaves and an inferior status for women, though Paul also writes an inspired letter to the Galatians in which he tells us, "There is neither Jew nor Greek, there is neither bond nor free, there is neither male nor female: for ye are all one in Christ Jesus" (Galatians 3:18). And we know there are other books not in our Protestant Bibles — "apocryphal," we call them; for we have fragments of at least fifty gospels in addition to the four we have preserved in our Bible.

But, again, as we read with discernment, as we listen to the church, we can understand the Bible quite well, thank you, to use it as our guide.

When we open our eyes we can readily see that the Bible is not only reflecting existing cultures, its own and ours, but also challenging them, turning them upside down, calling for a new and better way. In the end of all, our problem is less in *understanding* the Bible than in *living* it. JUST BELIEVE THE BIBLE.

So we need to THINK. Part of our discernment is our ability to reason, even our good old common sense—though what we call "common sense" is often a quite uncommon thing. This ability to reason, to think, to discriminate, to make things make sense—that is a gift of God, too, just as the church is, just as the Bible is. It is yet another way for us to understand what we should believe, how we should act. Let us, then, slap another bumper sticker on the backsides of our souls, this one reading, THINK. When John Calvin, at the peak of the Protestant Reformation, was running not only ecclesiastical life but everything else in Geneva, a builder of a new church edifice asked him the trivial question, "How high should a church door be?" Calvin replied, "High enough to bring your head in with you." THINK.

And try one that says, I FEEL IT IN MY SOUL. For our intuition, our feeling, is an important part of our knowing what is right. It is the "stuff" of the arts—all of which depend on a flow between clear thinking and the intuitive, imaginative, creative faculties for their substance and form. This is also the way we make our most important decisions: we *may* do a careful analysis of the good qualities and bad qualities of a potential husband or wife, assessing them very carefully and critically with our minds; but most decisions to marry are decisions of feeling, of intuition, of something deeper than thought. Just so, you love God with your mind, with your will, and also with your heart— your powerful feelings, your intuitive self.

The last bumper sticker I would plaster on my own soul reads, IT'S EXPERIENCE THAT COUNTS. When you read the Bible, cover to cover or even in snippets, what you find there are the stories, the histories of people who met God and walked with God in their *experience*. While Babylonians and Egyptians worshipped Nature as their gods and their kings as embodiments of those Nature gods, the Bible tells us about ordinary men and women experiencing God every day. God is a God of history, which means God is a God of experience. His "chosen people" were to teach their children in these words:

—
6

A wandering Aramean was my ancestor; he went down into Egypt and lived there as an alien, few in number, and there he became a great nation, mighty and populous. When the Egyptians treated us harshly and afflicted us, by imposing hard labor on us, we cried to the Lord, the God of our ancestors; the Lord heard our voice and saw our affliction, our toil, and our oppression. The Lord brought us out of Egypt with a mighty hand and an outstretched arm, with a terrifying display of power, and with signs and wonders; and he brought us into this place and gave us this land, a land flowing with milk and honey (Deuteronomy 26:5-9).

These are words of *experience*, the historical experience of a people.

"We were slaves. We asked God to deliver us. God heard our prayers. God showed his great power in bringing us out of our terrible condition. God brought us to this good and safe and plenteous land. We tell you this because it happened to us, it is our *experience*."

In like fashion you have your own personal experience: "On a day, in that place, at that time, I met Jesus as my savior and Lord." "On a day, when I needed help, God helped me." "On a day, at a place, at a time, at a moment in my life, God gave me the strength to endure, and not only to endure but to prevail. God delivered me." "On a day, God gave me the words to say that needed to be said." Experience. We know what to believe, we know how to act, in part through our *experience* of God. IT'S EXPERIENCE THAT COUNTS.

Well, by now we must feel that the backsides of our souls, the bumpers of our spiritual lives, are a mess. We wanted a simple, easy answer about what we should believe and how we should behave. And instead, we have five—count them, five—bumper stickers slapped on, stuck every which way, until we feel like our soul is an old 1925 Ford pickup (purchase price, new, $281), driven by Flem Snopes, with a mattress tied to the top of the cab and hound dogs in the back and five kids with runny noses looking out the windows.

But appearances are deceiving, thank God. The fact is, your soul, your spirit, with these five truths guiding your life, is a brand new spiritual Mercedes, top of the line. Just think about it: our lives are complex, complicated, even difficult. Does it stand to reason that any single source of insight, any one quick fix, will answer all the questions, solve all the problems, of our days?

No, not at all. And so we go to our church—LISTEN TO THE CHURCH; and to our Bibles—JUST BELIEVE THE BIBLE; and to our own reason and good sense—THINK; and to our intuitive center—I FEEL IT IN MY SOUL; and to our experience, and others' experience, of God— IT'S EXPERIENCE THAT COUNTS. And putting all these sources, all these authorities together, we find our way to God. And we take up our walk with God.

It is complex, of course—life is complex. We are not always sure we are right, of course—none of us ever is. But I would warrant you that if you listen to what you learn in church, obey what you read in the Bible, use your reason and good sense, follow your highest feelings, and rely on your experience of God, you will be right many more times than you will be wrong.

"Just tell me what to believe, and I'll believe it." Hey. I just did. It wasn't as simple as we might have wanted, but it is more real, more true. Church, Bible, reason and good sense, passion and noble feeling, our experience of God. Let them all play in your life as you walk with your Lord and you will not only *find* your way, but *lead* the way.

In the name of the God who always, always walks beside us,

Amen.

Pastoral Prayer

O God, it is all so complex, and we want it to be so simple.
Our lives get complicated, and mixed up, and messed up, and we don't
know what to do.
We get confused, and disturbed, and depressed, and we don't know
where to turn.
Others make life difficult for us, but not nearly so difficult as we make
it for ourselves.
And, we confess, we make life hard for them as well.

It is never easy, and we so want it to be easy.
It is never simple, and we so want it to be simple.

We want to rest and let the rivers of comfort and peace flow over us.
We are tired of fighting it, tired of working so hard, tired of failing, tired of trying.

And so, O God, in our frustration and despair, come to us and tell us how it is.
We know, in our heart of hearts, that we were made for the climb, that we are at our best when we are striving and prevailing.
Tell it to us straight, Lord. Tell us to Buck Up, to Snap Out of It, to Get a Life, to Face Reality, to Find the Promised Land of your mercy and grace and strength.
Let us hear it straight, and then let us come to you, and let us listen, and let us learn.

Teach us through these good people of the family of God, your church.
Teach us through Holy Scripture.
Teach us through our consecrated common sense, our reasoning and reasonable selves, our noblest intuitions, our highest passions, our richest experience of your justice and mercy and grace.
Teach us so we may be comforted, so we may be a comfort to others.

Bless those who are searching: may they find truth.
Bless those who are ill: may they find health.
Bless those who mourn: may they find peace.
Bless those who hunger: may they be filled.
Bless those who fall from the path: may they find your high way of goodness and truth.

Lord, have mercy.
Christ, have mercy.
Lord, have mercy.

Amen.

Saints and Begorra: God Is Close

"What Can We Really Believe?"
Theology in a Practical Key: Understanding God (Immanence)

Psalm 8. Psalm 8:1: "O Lord, our Lord, how majestic is your name in all the earth."

I wish to offer this morning's sermon out of some July weeks spent in Ireland, where we visit often and even own a little traditional Irish cottage, and in fact out of many years of reading about and participating in the Irish spirit of faith. This is not, however, a "what I did on my summer vacation" kind of sermon, and if the truth be known it was prepared before ever this journey happened.

Yet I do want to speak with you this morning about Celtic Christianity and what we may learn from it. In doing so, I continue a series of sermons on *What Can We Really Believe? Theology in a Practical Key*—for no religion is traditionally more practical and down to earth than the everyday faith of the folk-Irish. And we consider today an understanding of God, God as *immanent*, close to us, with us and in us—the kind of God the traditional Irish have worshipped in daily life.

This closeness of God experienced by our Irish brothers and sisters in their natural, instinctive faith can teach us two things, I think: (1) a wholeness we often lack and (2) a joy we often miss.

Let me try to explain this in a kind of bookish, academic, school-teacher-y way—after all, I did earn a doctor's degree in church history once and should use it sometimes—and then we will, as the kids might say, "get serious," " real."

American Christianity—the kind of religion we grew up with (as an English wit has said, "at our mother's knee or some low joint like that")—draws largely from two traditions, Roman Catholicism and Protestant Puritanism. Both have tended to separate the sacred and the secular, everyday life from religious life; and both have tended to be not just serious, but ascetic and grim.

You know what I'm talking about.

On the Catholic side, celibate priests and nuns denying themselves lives most mortals see as normal or natural; monks following intense spiritual disciplines; a rejecting of the flesh and its pleasures; worship services that for centuries were in a Latin language most people didn't even understand; a sharp separation between the clergy and the laity; huge guilt trips; a sense that religion is over *there* amidst the smoke of incense and the bells and the candles—"smells and bells," my Catholic friends like to say—while real life is over *here*.

But lest we get self-congratulatory and unctuous on the Protestant side, let me say that American Protestantism has been even grimmer. Early Puritans stalked sin in every form—read Nathaniel Hawthorne's *The Scarlet Letter* again. They held long, fierce worship services where a Jonathan Edwards would preach his classic sermon on "Sinners in the Hands of an Angry God"—just listen to that title—and where a Puritan diary could say, quite seriously, "Brother Smyth prayed a short prayer, about an hour it was." Waves of revivalism burnt over vast stretches of American geography in the nineteenth century, "purifying" simple folk in community bonfires of religious frenzy.

I myself grew up in a small-town Missouri church where we were enjoined not to go to movies, not to play cards, not to dance, not to indulge in what they called "mixed bathing," not to drink alcohol in any form, not to mess around with any kind of sex, not to smoke. My preacher-dad used to say, only partly in jest, "We don't smoke and we don't chew and we don't go with girls that do."

As with American Catholics, so with American Protestants: there was a whole bunch of "No" and Don't" in it, even a lot of anger along with truckloads guilt. It was religion-with-a-vengeance, a tightly controlled asceticism and self-denial over *there*, often separated from everyday life over *here*.

Roman Catholicism has over centuries imposed a lot of these characteristics on the Irish, who became—as they say—"more Catholic than the Pope." But even the grimmest, fiercest forms of religion-with-a-vengeance have not been able to overcome that native Celtic character which takes joy in life, in the world around us, in the God above us and in us. I see it every day when I am in Ireland. The Irish believers, when they are most themselves, are deeply spiritual and filled with a sense of awe, a sense of wonder. They can therefore teach us much about walking with God every moment of every day, about getting our lives together, making ourselves sole and whole, unifying what we call "spiritual" or "sacred" with what we call "secular." That is, to live the way Jesus taught us to live.

Let me explain by speaking briefly of **Place**, of **Time**, of **Actions**, and of **Persons**.

To the traditional Irish Christian, every place, every space, is filled with the presence of God. This sense of the spirit world living with us in our everyday world predates Christianity, to be sure—it is the pagan world of the *sidhe*, the "little people," the leprechauns, the spirits. Old Irishman P. J. McKenna told his family that these spirits could not be seen "straight on," but only out of the corner of the human eye, seen at a slant glance, as it were. Then when Christianity came to Ireland through St. Patrick's efforts, and the efforts of St. Brigid and St. Colmcille, these "everywhere spirits" became translated into God and the angels and the saints, now seen as loving, living spirits that are everywhere and in everything, for us.

So, God is in a beautiful house of worship like this, to be sure—in the church; but, to the Irish, God is also in the sun as it gleams, the wind as it blows, the ocean roaring or still, the stream running by the cottage door. And even more intimate and close, God is in the fire in our hearth, God is in our bedroom, at our table, in our car, at our desks, in our kitchens, in our classrooms, in our heads as we think, our lips as they speak or touch, our hearts as they feel, our hands and fingers as we work or create. God is with us as we turn on the computer, with us as we shop in the grocery store for the four basic food groups—Diet Pepsi, Wheat Thins, Cheese Whiz, and Ben & Jerry's Ice Cream, with us as we brush our teeth, with us as we put on our clothes or take them off, with us everywhere, all the time, at every moment.

That's why, as I can show you from books I hold and love, there is an Irish prayer for "Turning on the Light": *Savior, may you give the light of heaven to every poor soul who has left this life, and every poor soul who ever prayed.* A prayer for "Putting a Child to Bed": *God bless you child. I place you under the shadow of God's great love, under the cloak of Christ's care, under Holy Spirit's shelter. God be with you, little one, this night.* A prayer for "Blessing the Bed on Going to Sleep," for "Ending the Work Day." For "Lighting the Fire in the Morning," for "Milking the Cow," for "Fishing" — some of you want a copy of that last one, I know.

The point? We can learn from the Irish a great truth of faith: God is with us and in us, anywhere we are, everywhere we are. The smallest things are worthy of God's attention, of God's involvement, which of course makes it easier for God to be involved in the larger things of our lives, since he is involved in the small, the everyday. It is really quite beautiful.

So when the Irish ask, in their native language, if there is any news (we might say, "Hi, how ya doin'? What's up? What's goin' on, any news?) the question in the Gaelic language is quite literally this: "What are the great wonders today?" Why does the Irish language say it this way? Because if God is everywhere, if God is part of everything, then anything and everything is potentially a "great wonder."

I like this very much. Instead of being jaded, cynical, bored, calcified, numbed by the routine, sucked dry, rubbed to dead bone by the users of this world, brought to despair by the aimlessness and pointlessness that confronts us every day, we can live with a huge sense of wonder. God is everywhere! What, then, is today's marvel! What are the great wonders today? Everything has gone right today? Praise God for his gifts. Nothing has gone right today? Praise God, for it will be better soon. We can see, feel God in the warmth of a bed, the cool of water, the beauty of an opening flower, the song of a bird, the voice of a friend, the inner strength to prevail another day, in another person whom we can help, in the power and good sense to do the next right thing. For that's the essence of morality, isn't it? Not to make grand resolutions, not to concoct noble schemes, but simply to do "the next right thing."

We begin each day, live each day, lay our heads on our pillows at night, with a sense of wonder. A loving, caring, saving God is with us everywhere, always. I always thought the words of Jesus ending the Gospel of Matthew — "Lo, I am with you always, even to the end of the world" — were only about his earlier words commanding us to "Go, teach, baptize, make disciples." And of course the words *are* about our work for God. But I have learned from the Irish that these "comfortable words" are even bigger: when we are working for God, yes, he is with us always, even to the end of the world; but he is also with us always when we are resting, or playing, or loving, or weeping. The comfortable words, the true words: "Lo, I am with you always." A great wonder!

If God is with us every place, and at every moment—all the time—then we can relax in our Christian journey because it is not all depending on us. God is present, working with us and in us and for us, whether we are aware of it or not. This gives a new perspective on prayer: it is not just the words we make, but it is also what God is doing, "saying" on our behalf, as it were, as we rest in God's being there all the time. I now understand, from the Irish, those verses in Romans 8:26-27: "Likewise the Spirit helps us in our weakness; for we do not know how to pray as we ought, but that very Spirit intercedes with sighs too deep for words ['groanings which cannot be uttered']. And God, who searches the heart, knows what is the mind of the Spirit, because the Spirit intercedes for the saints according to the will of God." That is why the next verse can read, "We know that all things work together for good for those who love God." God is with us at every moment, whether we are thinking of him or not, and that is no small thing.

Down a steep path from our little cottage in Ireland, in the remote County Donegal village of Glencolmcille—Glen of St. Colmcille—"Glen of the Dove of the Church"—is a wide sandy beach at the head of Glen Bay. Not many days can you swim in Ireland without turning blue all over your body—part of the charm of the place is cool water, cool breezes—but on days when you can swim, the cool salt waters of the Atlantic buoy you up, and you float, and you are refreshed, and you are supported by the great ocean itself, and you are a small secure part of something larger and greater and good. You don't thrash the water to stay afloat, you don't beat the waves, you don't attack the universe; you simply rest yourself in the great sea, and it holds you up. So with our God. We rest in God, and God holds us up.

And the fact that every place and every moment of time are filled with God's presence gives the Irish believer, and can give us, great joy. God is here, now. Therefore let us rejoice. Let us celebrate. If it is a happy

---

time like a wedding, the Irish celebrate. If it is a sad time like a funeral, the Irish celebrate—a true Irish wake is a quite good party. Life is celebration, for God is, as they say, "in it." God is there.

That is one reason Irish prayers and blessings are often as whimsical as they are serious. There *are* such beautiful poetic blessings as, *May the road rise to meet you; may the wind be always at your back; may the sun shine warm upon your face, the rain fall soft upon your fields; and, until we meet again, may God hold you in the hollow of his hand.* But there are also fanciful, even quirky prayers like, *May you be in heaven an hour before the divil* [sic] *knows you're dead,* or, *May those who love us, love us; and those who hate us, may God turn their hearts; and if he won't turn their hearts, then may God turn their ankles, so we'll know them by their limping.* There is joy, fun, celebration in faith, for God is here, with us, in every place, in every moment of every day and every night.

This means that our actions are holy, for God is with us as we do them. Religious things, yes—like prayer and worship and singing hymns and giving our money or time or selves; but also everyday things like working and playing and loving and sleeping. And if every **place** is holy because filled with God's presence, and our **time** the same, and our **actions** also, it follows that **each of *us*** is holy to God, for each of us has God's presence with us and in us.

Even women? Oh, yes, especially women. Even children? Oh, yes. That's why *Roman* Catholicism had great difficulty placing only males in charge of the Irish church, for the traditional Irish had a sense that women and children were as important as men—we are all God's children, all sacred beings. The two greatest Irish saints are Patrick and Brigid, man and woman. An irony of church history is that the Roman Catholic ways of male dominance were adopted in the English speaking world at an important church conference, the Synod of Whitby in Celtic northern England in 664 AD, which was *not* presided over by a man—but get this—by St. Hilda, a woman, in whose abbey the meeting took place. This formidable woman ruled over both nuns *and* monks, women *and* men, and the Irish haven't forgotten it.

Differences between rich and poor, high and low, are not important. After all, God owns all things, and the rich person and poor person are equally good in God's eyes. The Gaelic language doesn't even have words for "my possession," what I own—the closest one gets is "my portion." Nothing is really mine, it all belongs to God, and this is "my portion."

There is a charming tale of St. Brigid who, having just convinced a local king to accept Christianity by working some powerful miracles—changing bath water into beer, in a miracle a few of you ornery Irishmen might appreciate, and mimicking Elijah and St. Patrick in calling down fire from heaven to put pagan Druid priests in their place—then went into the humblest cottage of the poorest family to tell them of Jesus. In explaining Jesus Christ to them, she bent down to pick up rushes from the dirt floor, wove them into the shape of a cross—I have one in my hand, woven in Ireland—and helped them see that Jesus loved them so much he died for them, helped them find salvation and a sense of God's loving care for their lives.

To this day many Irish will weave such crosses and put them over doors or windows, saying God is with us, protecting us, saving us in this house. A traditional Irish greeting on entering a room is "God save all here." High or low, rich or poor, God is with us, cares for us, loves us.

This is so today for you and me, even in this room, in this house of worship: the great God, the High King of Heaven, comes to each of us and says, "I am with you, in every place, at every moment, in every act, every deed you do. Whoever you are, whatever your place in life, woman or man or girl or boy, rich or poor, humble or powerful, you are holy to me, my child. You are one of my own."

Saints and Begorra. It doesn't get better than that.

Amen.

Pastoral Prayer

We offer to God this morning in the words of three ancient Irish prayers.

Bless to me, O God, each thing mine eye sees;
Bless to me, O God, each sound mine ear hears;
Bless to me, O God, each smell that goes to my nostrils.
Bless to me, O God, each taste that goes to my lips.
Bless this day, I pray,
 Each note that goes to my song,
 Each ray that guides my way,
 Each thing that I do with hands and strength,
 Each thing I do with heart and soul,
 Each thing I do with mind and will.
Save me this day, I pray, from
 Each lure that tempts my will,
O God that seeks my living soul.
O God that seeks my living soul.
Amen.

I arise today through strength of heaven,
 Light of sun,
 Radiance of Moon
 Splendor of Fire,
 Speed of Lightning,
 Swiftness of Wind,
 Depth of Sea,
 Stability of Earth,
 Firmness of Rock.
I am safe in you, O God, safe and strong and secure,
I give thanks to you, O God, forever and forever,
Amen.

May the blessed God enfold me,
May the blessed God surround me,
 May God be in my speaking,
 May God be in my thinking.
 May God be in my sleeping,
 May God be in my waking,
 May God be in my watching,

May God be in my hoping.
May God be in my life,
May God be in my lips,
May God be in my soul,
May God be in my heart.
May God be in my eating,
May God be in my slumber,
And may the blessed God save my ever-living soul,
Amen.

Benediction

May the road rise to meet you.
May the wind be always at your back.
May the sun shine warm upon your face.
And rains fall soft upon your fields.
And until we meet again,
May God hold you in the hollow of his hand.

Why Did They Call God a Guy?

"What Can We Really Believe?"
Theology in a Practical Key: Understanding God (Transcendence)

Isaiah 40:1, 10-18, 21-31.   Isaiah 40:25: "'To whom then will you liken me or shall I be equal?' saith the Holy One."

There is a hairy old story that made the rounds of seminaries and church institutions a good while back concerning an angel accidentally impaled on the nose cone of a space probe and, amazingly, coming to earth with the space capsule as it returned. This was an instant media event, medically and theologically and for the entire world; and as hospitals and physicians were experimenting with their angel medicines, trying to heal the celestial creature, a team of theologians led by an august seminary president was gathering around to ask questions about heaven and the afterlife and things beyond human knowledge.

After several tentative queries, the theologians finally dared the ultimate question, poising notepads and pens and recording machines and TV cameras to take notes and preserve the precious words while the seminary president screwed up his own blustery courage to ask it:

"Is there a God?"

"Yes," replied the shy and wounded angel. "There is a God."

Great relief all around. After all, with no God, the theologians and seminarians would have been out of a job.

Then the next question:

"What is God like?"

Pens still at ready, notepads still open, cameras and recording devices still whirring, the theologians waited for the answer. Would the angel emphasize omniscience, omnipotence, omnipresence, immanence, transcendence, spiritual force, ultimate being, absolute holiness? How would the angel describe God, in this only first-hand eyewitness account mortals had ever heard?

A long, long pause. The suspense built. The theologians strained every spiritual nerve, every brain cell.

Until finally the angel answered, ever so quietly, "She's black."

Now why, I ask, as I have thought about first hearing that story, why was it considered a gag, something funny?

Because humor resides in the unexpected, and because in the dominant images of Europe and North America, *He's White*." According to popular (if inaccurate) legend, Michelangelo lay on his back, on scaffolding, for four arduous years painting the ceiling of the Sistine Chapel in Rome and gave us, Ta-Da, the European-American's picture of God: a giant, muscular white male with long flowing white beard, a titan dressed in white robe, finger extended to send the spark of life across the chasm of the universe to an inert Adam and Eve: "Let there be life."

God, king of the heavens, giver of life, is to us a "he," and that "he" is "white."

Not to everyone, of course. I have viewed wonderful pictures of God, really of Jesus, as an Oriental, as an African, as a Native American, even as an Eskimo. All people tend to create God or gods in their own likenesses, and it is important to do so for reasons we shall soon explore. But in fact, we have no choice: we are forced to shape likenesses of God in our heads and words and carvings and paintings and songs, partly because there exists no other image of God.

God is spirit, God is holy, God is infinite, God is other — "wholly other," some theologians have told us. God is beyond us, past all understanding or finding out, beyond all grasping or cozying up to or domesticating. So, in this third sermon in the series *What Can We Really Believe? Theology in a Practical Key*, we seek to understand this "otherness": God's transcendence, God's majesty and greatness, and what that means for us.

The first thing it means, of course, is that God is mystery. One of Tom Stoppard's lesser-known but better plays, entitled ***Jumpers***, puts on stage a character named George, a philosopher, dictating a paper which debates the existence of God and speculates on the attributes of God — which may include, he says, "omniscience, perfection, and four-wheel drive." The philosopher struggles and struggles to explain God until finally in frustration he gives up, dictating to the stenographer, "Is God? — leave a space."

Now think about that: "Is God? — leave a space." What we can know of God, ultimately, is "The Space" — that God is mystery, greater than any of our explanations.

Because God is mystery, beyond our understanding, we necessarily speak of God in what we call "anthropomorphic" language — *anthropo* for "humankind," as in *anthropos*, *morphic* for "in the form of" — so, in the form of humankind. Thus the Bible speaks of God as walking in the garden in the cool of the day, or cutting a deal with Abraham over the destruction of Sodom and Gomorrah, or talking with Satan in the Book of Job and setting up a massive test of Job's faithfulness. Even in the first chapters of Genesis, as God is creating sun and moon and stars and oceans and rivers and fish and birds and animals and finally humankind, you get a sense of very human — that is, anthropo-morphic — delight as God creates something and says, "very good," then makes something else and says, "very good." "Wow, that's good. I like that. Very good." You can almost feel this God clapping hands in pleasurable joy.

Then, because the culture of the Bible is primarily patriarchal, male-dominated, it is only natural that God would be described in anthropomorphic terms as a guy, a very powerful guy, indeed, a patriarch — head of the human family, chieftain, king — king of the human race, king of all the earth. In a culture where men were lords and masters, where women were possessions and chattel, God had to be a man to fill the word pictures with the authority God has to have.

There is nothing particularly wrong with this so long as we understand why it happened and understand that the metaphor — God as a powerful man, a patriarch, a king — is just that — a metaphor, a figure of speech, and not a literal description of reality. The writers of the Bible were saying "God is *like* a powerful man," "God is *like* a ruler of the tribe," God is *like* a king."

21

When we were kids we used to say the word "plike" — for "play like," pretend. "Plike I'm a cowboy and you're and Indian," or "Plike I'm a teacher and you're a student," or "Plike I'm a fireman and you're a fire" — then the play got very creative. But it was important not to confuse "plike" with what was real. We were kids, playing. Even so in describing God as a guy, a big strong guy, it is important to recognize that it is "plike," a metaphor, a very high form of verbal play, but not a description of reality.

Thus a literalistic view that says men are to have dominance over women because God is male — that is dead wrong, elevating metaphor to reality, taking a symbolic expression and making it deadly serious. Same for the idea of refusing to ordain women, or not letting women speak in the church, or keeping women in any way subservient in family or society. This is bad theology, based on a bad understanding of God and Holy Scripture. It turns the *culture* of the Bible into *teachings* of the Bible, a very bad mistake.

The fact is, God is not a guy. Nor is God a gal. Nor is God a human in any form. "God is spirit," Jesus said, and those who worship God must worship "in spirit and in truth" (John 4:24).

Images of God in the Bible, in both the Hebrew and Greek languages, are sometimes feminine, sometimes masculine. Insofar as God has any kind of humanity or sexuality, the description would have to be "fullness," or "completeness" — embracing all of what we are, whoever we are, and all of what the world is. That is why, I think, the doctrine of the Trinity grew up — it was an effort to explain God in God's fullness and completeness — the heavenly God as father, the earthly God as Jesus, the present-with-us Holy Spirit, all taken together as an effort to begin to tender a whisper of a hint of a glimmer of a description of who God is. For, again, the fact of the matter is that, in some ways of being, God is transcendent, wholly other, beyond us. God is majesty, mystery, holiness, strength.

> Earlier theologians did try to explain God as "omnipotent, omniscient, omnipresent" — God is all powerful, God is all-knowing, God is all-present, everywhere at the same time. That is to say, he was totally "God." Not "a god," but "God."

Medieval theologians were fond of arguing God's existence, "proving" him by reasonings such as the *teleological* argument—God must exist because there is design in the universe. Carl Jung, the great psychiatrist, echoed this argument when he said that the possibility of this universe occurring without God's existing and God's creating it is the same possibility as an unabridged dictionary's being formed from an explosion in a print shop.

Or the *ontological* argument—God must exist because, as the philosophers said, "God is the presupposition of the question of God"; if God doesn't exist you couldn't ask the question of whether God exists, therefore even the atheist is really a believer because if there were no God then there would be nothing in which the atheist could disbelieve.

These arguments were all presented to God once, as I understand it— "God, are you the root and ground of being, the ultimate essence, the presupposition of the question of God, the wholly other, the primal cause, the unmoved mover."

And God, as I understand it, answered, "Huh?"

Discussing the attributes of God and arguing the existence of God may intrigue scholars, keep theologians employed, and drive students mad, but it is like reading that the sun will burn itself out in five billion more years or so—it is hard to take it very personally.

What are important to us are the two things that drove people to describe God as a guy in the first place: first, God is powerful, all powerful; and second, God cares for us, is with us, looks after us.

That was the image of the patriarch in the Bible: power and care. He would make the decisions on where the family and tribe could live safely—*power*; would and could defend from attacks of other tribes or warlords—*power*; would and could lead out in making flocks and herds and crops to grow—*power*; would nurture and feed and protect and comfort and sustain his family, his herds, his tribe—*care*.

Translated to our life and our times, we also understand God as **power** and **care**. We pray to God because we believe in God's power, God *can*

23

do something to help us. And we pray to God because we believe in God's care—God *will* do something to help us. Jesus said it, as some of his last words to his disciples: "All power is given unto me in heaven and in earth—*power*; and lo, I am with you always, even to the end of the world—*care*." And it was Jesus who most helped us understand that the compassion of God is our salvation, our access to a loving relationship with God through all our lives.

Here, for the Christian, is the most amazing and marvelous thing: that this transcendent God, God above us, God beyond us, God of power and might and majesty and mystery and magnificence, that this all-powerful God takes notice of each of us, knows us by name, loves us, cares for us, looks after us. If God wanted to and *couldn't* care for us, he would be no God. If God could care for us and *wouldn't*, he would be no God as we know him in Jesus Christ. But both are there—majesty and love, power and care.

This means we have access to a strength beyond our own that is greater than any trial, any problem, any pain, any defeat, any reversal, even death itself.

And so we pray, "Our Father who art in heaven, hallowed be thy name," and this great and holy God hears us and comes to our aid even in the most basic of things: "Give us this day our daily bread."

The fortieth chapter of Isaiah is a remarkable section of scripture, one of the great "purple passages" of Holy Writ, perhaps my favorite in all the Bible. It speaks of God's transcendence, God above us, his power and might, greater than any we could ever imagine: "'To whom then will ye liken me, or shall I be equal?' saith the Holy One" (v. 25). God "measured the oceans in the hollow of his hand and measured out heaven with his ruler" (v. 12). He is instructed by no one, takes counsel from no one—he is God and needs no teaching (vv. 13-14). To him, the nations "are as a drop of a bucket and are counted as the small dust on the scales" (v. 15); rulers and kings he brings to nothing, they are vain emptiness (v. 23). God made the stars and sun and moon, weighs the mountains in his scales, holds all the dust of the earth in his measuring cup (vv. 26, 12). This is a picture of God above us, great and powerful and mighty.

But this very same chapter, Isaiah 40, *begins* with these words, "Comfort ye, comfort ye my people" (v.1). Just after the powerful words about an all-powerful God in verse 10, "Behold, the Lord God will come with strong hand, and his arm shall rule for him: behold his reward is with him, and his work before him" —just after these words of transcendence and strength come the comforting, "comfortable words" that define God's work: "He shall feed his flock like a shepherd: he shall gather the lambs with his arm, and carry them in his bosom, and shall gently lead those that are with young" (v. 11).

Ah, this is magnificent. The great God of the universe, the wholly other, the all-powerful creator of all that is, has taken as his task the tender care of his lambs, of you and me, whom he gathers into his strong and gentle bosom with his strong and gentle hands, tenderly leading "those that are with young."

Small wonder, then, that this great text of Isaiah 40 would come to a climax in the soaring words,

> Hast thou not known? Hast thou not heard, that the everlasting God, the Lord, the Creator of the ends of the earth, fainteth not, neither is weary? There is no searching of his understanding.

> He giveth power to the faint; and to them that have no might he increaseth strength.

> Even the youths shall faint and be weary, and the young men shall utterly fall:

> But they that wait upon the Lord shall renew their strength; they shall mount up with wings as eagles; they shall run, and not be weary; and they shall walk, and not faint (vv. 28-31).

God is God.

God is Love.

Thanks be to God!

Amen.

Pastoral Prayer

All Mighty God,

We don't even know how to approach your majestic throne, so high
and lifted up are you.

You shaped the stars and hung them in space;
You lit the sun with fire and made it our light, our warmth;
You chose to mold our little planet Earth and bring us to life upon it,
such as we are.

You are great; we are small.
You are mighty; we are weak.
You know in full; we know in part.
You govern worlds; we do well to manage our little days.
You drive the planets in their rounds; we stick our noses in our iPads to
check the weather.

In our smallness, we bow before you
humbly, meekly, weakly, tentatively, hopefully, fearfully.
Yet we *do* bow before you,
coming to your throne of grace because you invite us to come, even
to "come boldly."
You tell us, and show us again and again,
that the face of your strength and power for us is your forgiving
love, your fatherly goodness.

Even this we do not fully understand;
We simply accept, in gratitude and trust.

Send your power, then, O mighty God, to show us our way and to lead
us in it.

Send your power, O God, to forgive us our trespasses.

Send your power O God, to bring health where there is sickness.

Send your power, O God, to offer the balm of peace where there is grief
or turmoil.

Send your power, O God to strengthen us in our weakness.

    Stiffen us in our resolve.
    Humble us in our wrongful pride.
    Empower us to do your work.

Send your power, O God, we earnestly pray,

Amen.

Jesus the Great

"What Can We Really Believe?"
Theology in a Practical Key: Understanding Jesus Christ (Christology)

Matthew 16:13-15. Matthew 16:16: "Simon Peter answered, 'You are the Messiah [the Christ], the Son of the living God.'"

I am not given to recommending books, or to lending them. Either can do one ill. In the first instance, you lose any reputation you might have for intelligence if the person doesn't like the book you recommend. In the second instance you simply lose the book. Literally dozens of my lent opinions, and my lent books, are at this moment floating around various cities and states and countries, none of them valued to any apparent degree by the recipient.

Yet today I dare to risk all by recommending to you three books that many of you will already know: they are by Thomas Cahill, the first three of a projected series of seven called "The Hinges of History," and they express the thesis of author Cahill that history is not only to be descried in acts of catastrophe, war, and outrage, but that history can also be what he calls "narratives of grace," events and movements that create the good.

His first book—appropriate for an Irish-American author named Cahill—is entitled *How the Irish Saved Civilization,* and it quite seriously demonstrates how Christianity and classical learning were preserved in the monasteries of remote Ireland during the fifth century when the dark ages had descended on Europe.

His second book, *The Gifts of the Jews,* describes the miracle of "how a tribe of desert nomads changed the way everyone thinks and feels," bringing us belief in the one God Jehovah, a high ethical code based on justice and mercy, and a sense of purpose to life and history.

His third book, *Desire of the Everlasting Hills,* helps us understand the uniqueness of Jesus Christ: "Who is Jesus Christ?" "What does Jesus Christ mean to me and to this world."

All three books are quite readable, informed by good scholarship, reasonably short, and worth taking to mind and heart. Thomas Cahill—try your favorite bookstore or Amazon.com. Thus endeth the commercial.

I speak at length on these three books (and there are others in the series as well), first because they are good, and second because they can teach much more than the scant twenty minutes of any sermon could ever teach. I also mention them because I am drawing on Cahill's third book, the one on Jesus, in today's consideration of the doctrine called "Christology"—Christ-ology—in our series on *What Can We Really Believe? Theology in a Practical Key.*

"Jesus the Great." Not a term we ever hear or heard, is it. Don't you find that strange? Jesus is called in scriptures the Son of Man—suggesting one with us, identifying with our humanity; and the Son of God—suggesting one with God, God in flesh; and *Messiah*—a Jewish word meaning "God's anointed one"; and *Christ*—a Greek word meaning the same thing, "God's chosen one." And even, in derision, "the King of the Jews," in a sign nailed with him to his cross.

But never "Jesus the Great."

There was an Alexander the Great. Born three hundred years before Jesus, in the province of Macedonia in a remote corner of Greece, Albania, and Serbia, he was called "great" because he was a brilliant general by age eighteen, king of Greece by age twenty, and master of the entire known world by age thirty. He broke the great empires of Persia and Egypt on his march to world conquest and then, it is said, sat down and wept because there were no worlds left for him to conquer.

Now he began, as the old folks used to say, "to put on airs." Power tends to corrupt, and absolute power tends to corrupt absolutely. Conquered peoples of Egypt declared him the "son of god," he founded multiple cities named "Alexandria" in his own honor, and in Babylon he was declared "king of kings" and began to dress and act like it. He behaved with incredible cruelty, by our modern standards, sending thousands to their deaths with just a word of personal whim. It still happens in that part of the world.

—

29

He finally met resistance in Bactria and Sogdiana, modern-day Afghanistan and Uzbekistan—again, the centuries haven't changed things all that much; his army deserted him in Pakistan, only one-fourth of them surviving the march home across the great deserts. Alexander himself became target of palace corruptions and intrigues, and he died in Babylon—yes, Babylon—in June of 323 B.C., just weeks short of his thirty-third birthday.

Despite the carnage he wreaked, the people of his age and most subsequent ages have seen in him enormous greatness, for he was a truly inspired and inspiring warrior-prince. He was a thinker and organizer as well as a warrior. He was a genius at "public relations," at image-building—particularly his own image. In addition to his brilliance in war, he loved learning—he slept with two objects under his pillow, a sharp dagger and a copy of Homer's *Iliad*; and he established libraries all over the world, the one at Alexandria in Egypt containing, it was said, "all the books of the world." He made Greek the universal language and culture of the known world, including that magnificent body of Greek art and literature. Because of his brilliance, he was called in his own time and since "the Great," "the greatest man who had ever lived," they said, the measure of man himself.

He was the standard. When Julius Caesar came along, he was considered an Alexander reborn. As was Augustus Caesar. And even pitiful old Herod out in Jerusalem, an Alexander wannabe, ruling as a puppet for three decades, living in a lavish marble palace and rebuilding a lavish temple not for God's glory but for his own. Herod, too, wanted to be "the Great" and even called himself such, this cruel man who lived for wealth and power, for pomp and place, for riches and self-centered display.

What is important for us today is that these were the images in Jewish minds as they waited, expectantly, for the promised Messiah and got instead a carpenter from Nazareth ("Can any good come out of Nazareth?") In their minds, the one coming would be "Messiah the Great," a second Alexander or King David, running the Roman legions out of town, restoring the power and the glory to Israel, taking over those lavish palaces and temple, returning pride and self respect to a conquered people. The Messiah would kill the enemies of Israel, destroy them utterly. He would be one tough dude, this Messiah the

Great. So, when people began calling Jesus "Messiah" — probably because they saw him working supernatural miracles — they meant him to be a Jewish Alexander the Great who would deliver his people by battle, just as their Joshua had done eleven or twelve hundred years before. (Jesus and Joshua are, in fact, different forms of the same name.)

So Jesus of Nazareth was to become Jesus the Great, a second Joshua, or a King David, or an Alexander, to lead the armies of Israel, to kill, to destroy, to obliterate the Romans in some "mother of all battles" and deliver his people to political freedom. Raw, naked physical power and military/political brilliance were on order. The hope of Israel at the time of Jesus was not for teachers of wisdom, not for preachers, but for visceral, primitive warrior-killers and leaders of legions.

This hope for a political warrior-leader was in the minds even of the twelve disciples, those closest to Jesus. It is why they couldn't get it — kept on not getting it — as Jesus spent time not with the big people, generals and kings, but with the poorest of the poor, teaching and helping and healing and feeding those who needed help. If Jesus were Messiah, as they believed, surely he would at some critical moment — Superman-like — throw off his ragged provincial carpenter-peasant clothes, put on the golden armor of an Alexander, and lead the revolution that would bring freedom. Even after his death on the cross, when in his resurrected person he came to them in Jerusalem, they asked him, "Lord, is this the time when you will restore the kingdom to Israel?" (Acts 1:6) Still, still, even after the cross, they expected a political hero, a warrior hero, a Jesus the Great.

Now of course there was more than a hint of self-interest in all this. There always is. James and John asked him, or perhaps their good Jewish mother asked for them — the narratives differ just a bit in Matthew and Mark's Gospels — if the two might sit one on his right hand and one on his left when he came into his kingdom. Mr. Prime Minister and Mr. President, right hand and left, corner offices in that fancy marble palace, with hot and cold running servants. Jesus would be king, Jesus the Great, and would carry his closest followers to power and glory with him. It had happened before, and it still happens today in the Middle East and other of what we call the "trouble spots" of the world.

But, of course, that is not what Jesus was all about. And that is why it was so hard for them to "get it," so hard for us to get it today. The teaching of Jesus, the life and death of Jesus, the Way of Jesus runs counter to our natural instincts to grasp for wealth and power, our natural tendencies to look out for old Number One, our selfish tendencies to ignore others in order to get what we want.

Look at the story in the New Testament. As just a plain old story it is full of delicious ironies and reversals. Jesus arrives on the scene, and the first words he speaks in the first written Gospel, that of St. Mark, are these: "The time is fulfilled, and the kingdom of God has come near ['is at hand']" (Mark 1:15). When he says this, his hearers expected revolution, for these were code words used in the prophets, in temple and synagogue, in teachings of rabbis, in the folk frenzy of the times, to say that the Messiah has come to restore the kingdom to Israel. These hearers quite naturally and quite understandably expected war, all-out warfare, or guerrilla warfare, or at least suicide stabbers (no bombs yet) to make a statement against Rome. Dozens of self-styled "messiahs" had already presented themselves asking for a following, so great was the Jewish yearning, even hysterical desire, for freedom. Here, at last, was Jesus the Great.

But after raising that flag of Jewish hopes, Jesus turns it all upside down in order to get at something much bigger and much more important than a political battle between a conquering and conquered people.

His next words are "repent" — probably that should be translated, "open your hearts." "Repent," and "believe the good news — the gospel." He is saying, "Be open to a new way of seeing things — open your hearts." And he is saying, "Believe this good news, this gospel: God is not just for the higher-ups, the Alexander the Greats, the Augustus Caesars, the Herod the Greats of the world, but God is for the poor and oppressed, and the common folk, even you and me.

Now that *is* good news in a world where the poor and weak have always suffered. Every day you and I pay attention to the rich and powerful, work to *become* the rich and powerful, and tend to ignore or avoid the poor and needy. Is it possible that God is paying attention to those who *need* and not just those who *have*? This was the revolutionary message Jesus taught.

See the Beatitudes of Matthew 5, part of what we call the Sermon on the Mount, and compare them with what Alexander the Great, or you or I, might have said.

> Blessed [Happy] are the poor in spirit: for theirs is the kingdom of heaven . . . .
> Blessed are the meek: for they shall inherit the earth.
> Blessed are they which do hunger and thirst after righteousness: for they shall be filled.
> Blessed are the merciful: for they shall obtain mercy.
> Blessed are the pure in heart: for they shall see God.
> Blessed are the peacemakers: for they shall be called the children of God . . . .

Alexander, or most of us, would have thought and taught, and we still think and teach, "Blessed, Happy, is the one who is rich and powerful. To be happy, you must have power. To be happy, you must have plenty. To be happy, you must make people do what you want them to do. To be happy, you must be in charge, in control, whatever it may take."

Of course, it doesn't really work out that way. We know lots of miserable folk who are both rich and powerful, and we know from observation and experience that you don't buy blessedness, happiness, joy. Over against this selfish way of life Jesus taught simple goodness. The phrases are worth hearing and reading again: "Blessed are the poor in spirit, Blessed are the merciful, Blessed are the pure in heart, Blessed are they who hunger and thirst after righteousness."

What a shocker.

In a world where Alexander was "the Great," the icon of what a person should be; in a place and time when Jesus's own people were expecting a Messiah who would act like Alexander, bringing war and judgment, power and glory, loot and booty, riches and prominence to his followers; Jesus said instead, "Turn it all on its head and look at it another way: depend on God; look after those who need our help; everyone is important, not just the rich and famous; all of us are God's children, all of us have a place in God's kingdom; all of us can be God's own servants in this world."

33

Jesus did not speak of war and killing, of cruelty and manipulation, of controlling people, of threats. Instead he spoke of loving one another and caring for those who need us. If you do *these* things, said he, you will be blessed, happy. These are, in fact, the *only* ways to blessing and happiness.

Small wonder the disciples couldn't get it. It just wasn't the way people did things. Small wonder we don't get it. It is just not the way people do things. It is truly revolutionary — a revolution that takes place inside our own spirits, one by one by one.

Quite literally, Jesus changed the world. And quite literally, Jesus can change your life and mine. We can be freed from our greed, our lust for control, our pride, our will to power. We can live a life of goodness and love, making a difference in the lives of those who need us, those around us.

And so we pray each Sunday, first saying words that honor the King of All Creation and signing up for his army — "Our Father, who are in heaven,/ Hallowed be thy name. Thy kingdom come, thy will be done." In terms of our life and times, the values of ours or any culture, this would mean greed and power, taking control, getting the Big Man's wishes done. But then it is all reversed, magnificently; and knowing what Jesus the *truly* Great meant by "Thy will be done," and knowing what the Kingdom of our Lord and of his Christ *really* is "on earth as it is in heaven," our words turn into humble thanks that we can be alive — "Give us this day our daily bread"; and humble appeals that we may be both forgiven and forgiving — "And forgive us our debts, as we forgive our debtors."

"Father forgive. Help us to be forgiving. Give us our life day by day, and give us spiritual strength."

As I say, these humble words come from Jesus the *truly* Great as he seeks to instill true greatness and goodness in you and me. Let us hear him. Let us believe him. Let us resolve to follow him. And then, sitting where we are, let us pray reverently, pray sincerely, these words of humility, these words of strength, these words of love:

Our Father, who art in heaven,
Hallowed be thy name.
Thy kingdom come, thy will be done,
On earth as it is in heaven.
Give us this day our daily bread,
And forgive us our debts, as we forgive our debtors.
And lead us not into temptation but deliver us from evil:
For thine is the kingdom, and the power, and the glory forever.
Amen.

Pastoral Prayer

Dear Lord Jesus Christ,

Our friend and brother, our savior and Lord,

Come to us as you came to your disciples and friends in the long ago.

Come to our homes, bless the food on the table, bless the chores to be done, bless the work of cleaning and washing up and fixing and tending and mending, bless the children at play, bless the neighbors who visit, bless those who gather around because they sense that you are present;

Come to our neighborhoods, our urban villages where we live, our farms and towns and communities, and help us live as neighbors and friends who care for one another;

Come to our streets and alleys and lanes and offer your blessing of safety, even of quiet; come to our shops and offices and bless those who are agents of grace not greed; come to our schools and bless those who teach and learn; come to our hospitals and bless those who minister and those who recover; come to our death days and spread your great mantle of love over all who grieve; come to our churches and temples and teach your holy word.

And, dear Lord Jesus, we pray that you will come to our own hearts.

We are caught in our sin; forgive us.
We are tormented in our sickness, our depression, our failures; strengthen us.

We are yearning for love; love us.
We want good things to do with our lives; use us in your service.

Thank you, Lord Jesus, for bringing your greatness as God to our everyday lives, as our friend, our brother, our savior, our Lord,

Amen.

Paraclete: Walking with God, and God Walking with Us

"What Can We Really Believe?"
Theology in a Practical Key: Understanding the Holy Spirit (Pneumatology)

Romans 8:26-28. **Romans 8:26:** "Likewise the Spirit helps us in our weakness."

"In the beginning God created the heavens and the earth. And the earth was without form, and void; and darkness was upon the face of the deep. And the spirit of God moved upon the face of the waters. And God said, Let there be light: and there was light" Genesis 1:1-3).

So read the first four sentences of the Holy Bible. The very first words of Holy Scripture, like, it's important! And aren't the images remarkable? Close your eyes, and let your minds picture the scene.

First, images of The Void. It is Formless. It is Dark. It is The Deep. Our eyes see a roiling chaos, like from a John Milton poem, or from a movie named Jurassic something or other. Our ears hear words like Tennyson's, "Chaos, Cosmos! Cosmos, Chaos!" Dark slime oozes up from bottomless pits, staining a pocked, pitted landscape, or soulscape. Fierce winds break up giant mountains, drive stones like hail before them. Flames singe, then sear all in their path. Oceans boil, vaporous rivers burn away banks like acid, poisonous steam explodes from black caves, skies are rancid with vapors, all the earth groans in travail. It is a picture of the earth before God's Spirit touches it with creative order. It is, metaphorically and symbolically, a picture of our souls, our lives, when we are in that personal chaos before God touches our lives with creative order.

And then? And then? The next words bring calm: "And the spirit of God moved upon the face of the waters. And God said, Let there be light: and there was light." No longer chaos, but in its place Clear, Brilliant Radiance. A quiet moving of God's Spirit over all this deadly, demonic, impenetrable chaos and old night; God's Spirit bringing Light to our souls, to our lives, to the world. And now comes Order and Creation, Life itself, step by step it comes, with all its Harmonies, Discipline, Law, Beauty.

As the priest and poet Gerard Manley Hopkins described it,

> The world is charged with the grandeur of God . . . .
> [Therefore, in the earth]
> There lives the dearest freshness deep down things;
> And though the last lights off the black West went
> Oh, morning, at the brown brink eastward, springs —
> Because the Holy Ghost over the bent
> World broods with warm breast and with ah! Bright wings.

Just as did the poets, so do I reverence these images from the Bible, am in awe of them. In a sense, these opening words of the Bible tell the whole story of our world, and of your life, and mine, all in a scant three verses:

> First, all is darkness, chaos, confusion — we are mixed up and messed up. Are you ever mixed up and messed up?

> Then, the Spirit of God moves over us in gentle, calm, loving strength. Have you let God's Spirit do that yet in your life?

> And then, all becomes right. We have new life, order, light, peace, purpose. Has that yet happened in you?

Now, I ask you, isn't that what we want? Don't we want it in our world? Don't we want it in our lives? A sense of Order. Of Peace. Of Purpose. New Strength. New Understanding — that is, Light? Well, let me tell you on this Sunday morning, we are blessed, for this is exactly what the Holy Spirit, the Spirit of God, can do and does, for us.

This is where God comes close. This is where it happens for us — or doesn't. We might be able to keep God the Father at arm's length, may in fact not be able to relate to this figure very personally at all. For many of us, God is "out there," or "up there" — again, Michelangelo's monumental figure painted on the Sistine ceiling — remote, distant, powerful, a bit threatening, forbidding, unapproachable. You might have difficulty connecting with "Almighty God, Our Heavenly Father."

And it might be difficult for many moderns to understand Jesus the suffering Galilean, who indeed brings us God's love and salvation but also seems somehow far away, wearing a robe and sandals and walking ancient Judean hills, saying things to his disciples that even *they* can't understand, let alone ourselves two thousand years later.

The Spirit of God, though—ah, in this Spirit, God is close. We can *feel* the Spirit. In the person of this Holy Spirit, God comes deep into our lives, into our heart of hearts; and we in turn come deep into the heart of God. Through the Holy Spirit, we are touched, changed, made different in our inner selves. Here, God is around us, within us, beside us, as close as our breath, as close as the breeze that caresses or the wind that drives. The Holy Spirit of God is present, immediate, here.

Now that's a good thing! We need God, we need Jesus, and through this Holy Spirit we can have God/Jesus/Spirit walking with us, even living inside our lives—"in our hearts," we say. Thanks be to God.

One way to understand this third person of the Trinity, as we seek to do at least a bit in this morning's sermon, part of a series on *What Can We Really Believe? Theology in a Practical Key*, is to ask, "What does this Holy Spirit of God bring to our lives?"

And the first answer is "Life itself." **Life**. Apart from God there is no life. This precious gift, the breath in your lungs, the beating of your heart, your awareness, your intelligence, your feeling, your warmth, your very being are from God! We read that God breathed into humankind the "breath of life and man became a living soul" (Genesis 2:7). *Breath* and *spirit* are the same word in the Hebrew language. It is so astonishing we can scarcely grasp it: God's Spirit gives us our very life. His breath is our breath.

But there is more. As the Bible teaches us, God's Spirit also brings order, harmony, the banishing of chaos from our souls. That is to say, the Spirit of God gives **Purpose** to our lives. We want that, don't we, miss it deeply when it is not there.

Say you are a young person looking to the future, asking, "What shall I, what should I, do with my life?" You are a man or woman successful in business or profession, skilled and smart and talented, yet something important is missing, and you find yourself looking about you, saying, "Isn't there more to life than this? What can I do to make a *real* difference in this world?" You are a mother and wife with many talents, perhaps you left a career to marry, you have invested fully in your children who are now growing up and feel they need you less, your husband is totally involved in work, and you say, "What do I do now? What is my purpose? How can I matter, make a difference?" Or you are an older person who has completed your greatest years of service through a career, and now you feel sort of on the shelf, knowing you have great wisdom and experience built up over a lifetime but no outlet, no use for it, no place to share it. "What is my purpose now?" you ask.

When we ask these questions, God's Spirit comes to us to say quite directly, "Ah, I do have a purpose for you. I have much to do in this world, and I need you. Others need you. Be my partner, help do my work."

I tell you outright these two things, as your minister of the morning, as one who has lived long and who has experienced what I am saying to you:

First, you must *seek* that purpose, using your intelligence and good sense, preparing yourself in every way to be ready and apt.

And second, you must patiently *wait for* that purpose. Our calling usually finds us, rather than our finding it. But listen, patiently listen, and you will hear it. Jesus told his disciples to do the hardest thing of all, to *wait* in Jerusalem after the traumatic, shocking events of his crucifixion, resurrection, and ascension — to *wait*, patiently. But then he made good on his word, "You shall receive power when the Holy Spirit has come upon you; and you shall be my witnesses [do my work, find your purpose], in Jerusalem, and in all Judea and Samaria, and to the ends of the earth" (Acts 1:8).

A respected woman in this congregation mused with me on her own search for a focus and a clear sense of purpose. Then, in inspiring words, she described putting two and two together and getting not four, but four hundred measures in blessings as she said, "Hey, we have people in this church who love to sing. And we have people who

---

take communion to care centers and shut-ins. What if small groups of us would go along to sing as communion is offered?" And, pow, wow, the Spirit works, and a great ministry is waiting to happen. God has a purpose for you, the highest purpose in the world — to do his work.

One of those huge British imperial "companies" offered a huge salary to an early missionary to Burma, a man with valuable knowledge of local language and culture and leaders, wanting him to open up that region for their trading (and no doubt ultimately their control). The missionary refused a salary more than a hundred times his current income, and the Governor General was puzzled: "What's the matter?" he asked. "Not enough money?" "No," came the humble and thoughtful answer, "It's just not enough job." God's work is great work, noble work, whether it is in the shaping of a nation or in the taking of communion and song to a local care home.

Life. **Purpose**. And what else does the Spirit of God create in us? Ah, simple **Goodness**. First, as Scripture teaches, the Spirit convicts us of our sin (John 16:8), then brings us to repentance, then leads us to conversion through faith in Jesus Christ. As Jesus said to Nicodemus, "except a person be born of water and of the Spirit, he cannot see the kingdom of God" (John 3:5).

After this, when we are walking the Christian walk, the Spirit keeps working in us to engender what the Bible calls the "fruits of the Spirit." Ephesians 5:9 describes these fruits, these qualities: "The fruit of the Spirit is in all goodness and righteousness and truth." Galatians 5:22-23 goes further: "The fruits of the Spirit [that is, the qualities God would grow in us] are love, joy, peace, patience, gentleness, goodness, faith, humility, judgment." And in a wry but wise understatement St. Paul concludes, "Against such there is no law."

This describes what we want to be, doesn't it: we *want* to be good, we *want* to be righteous, we *want* to be truthful, full of love and joy and peace and patience and faith. And how does this come about? We give ourselves, you give yourself, to the Holy Spirit's leading in your life, for these fruits are what God's Spirit creates in your character.

I heard a deacon once, in a little country church, describe another man as "good people." "He's good people." Whereupon a dear sister who

---

41

sort of made it her business to tell everyone else how to think and act—every church, big or small, has at least one--retorted, in a much-too-typical snit, "You are not supposed to judge whether someone is good or not, Harold." And the patient deacon answered, "I'm not being a judge, Emma; I'm just a fruit inspector." The fruits of God's Spirit are goodness and righteousness and truth.

Life. Purpose. Goodness. And finally, and quite simply, the Holy Spirit of God looks after us, cares for us. So, **Care.**

Jesus told his disciples, in John 14 and again in John 16, that he had to go away, but he would send the "Comforter," "that he may abide with you forever, even the Spirit of truth" (John 14:16-18). The word *Comforter*, Jesus' name for the Holy Spirit in this instance, is the Greek word *Paraclete*, literally, "one called alongside to help." The Spirit is with us, is in us, is God looking after us as "one called alongside to help." The refrain of the old hymn goes around in my mind:

And He walks with me, and He talks with me,
And He tells me I am his own;
And the joy we share as we tarry there,
None other has ever known.

Because Jesus sends this spirit of Care, he could tell his disciples, and tells us, "Let not your heart be troubled" (John 14:1); "Peace I leave with you; my peace I give unto you" (John 14:27).

Most of you have heard, in person or film or recording, the late great tenor Luciano Pavarotti, who presented his American recital debut in a program of a college I formerly served as president, William Jewell College [in Liberty, MO], and who then returned four times during my tenure there for performances in the great arts series sponsored by that school. The morning after his tenth anniversary recital, our college awarded in convocation an honorary doctor of music degree to "The Great One," who stood resplendent in his very large academic robes on the stage of Gano Chapel at William Jewell as I presented his diploma (hand engrossed in Latin) and carefully placed a doctoral hood over his head and across his shoulders, the velvet and silk of that academic symbol almost as luxuriant as his voice. Our students loved him and cheered him with great warmth.

After the convocation, Pavarotti came over to my office, took off that splendid academic robe, became informal in a kind of fishing jacket and cap, and sat with me talking about his experience of the place. The students had applauded their own professors with warmth nearly equal to their reception of Pavarotti. This puzzled him, for, as he told me, he had known nothing like this in Italy, where his college was an urban high rise and his teachers were remote, frightening authority figures who seldom knew the name of even a single student. Then he stepped over to the window of my office and looked out on the campus quadrangle, saw students chatting with one another and with their teachers, saw the lovely red-brick buildings accented by the ivy climbing up the side of Jewell Hall, the luxurious green grass of quadrangle and hillsides, the flags celebrating the day in the gentle breeze, the slant of autumn sun across that idyllic hilltop, the skyline of Kansas City etched on the horizon twelve miles distant. And he turned and said in his heavily accented English, "I love this place—it has a spirit all its own. It has Life." Then, a long pause, as he looked out the window again, and I heard that magnificent voice murmuring softly, almost under his breath, "It's beautiful. It's beautiful."

Just so, and a thousand times more, the Spirit of your self, the Spirit of your life, if you will have him, is the loving Holy Spirit of God, who will be with you, who will be in you, if you will but open the door. And if you *will* invite God in, someday, somewhere, someone will say of your life, "It's beautiful! It's beautiful!"

We sing it often:

> Praise God, the source of all our gifts!
> Praise Jesus Christ, whose power uplifts!
> Praise the Spirit, Holy Spirit!
> Alleluia! Alleluia! Alleluia!

Amen

Pastoral Prayer

O, Holy Spirit of God,

We so want to be good, to do good,
   to make a difference with our lives,
   to matter to someone, and to you.

O, Holy Spirit of God,

We so want to have order in our souls, our minds.

O, Holy Spirit of God,

We want to have strength in time of need,
   comfort in time of sorrow,
   hope in time of despair.
And we sometimes don't know how,
   even when we try.
And so we pray for help,
   that you will come to us as you promised.

Come to us as a Dove, bringing peace to our souls.
Come to us as a rushing mighty wind, bringing power to our lives and
      our words.
Come to us as tongues of fire, bringing truth to our days.
Come as our friend, our advocate, our comforter, our strength.
But come.

We thank you that you care for us, every moment.
We thank you that you care for all your children, moment by moment.
We thank you that you care for us when we are sick in body,
   despairing in spirit, struggling in our souls.
We thank you that you strengthen us,
   pick us up again,
   set us on the road afresh,
   lead us into the future as our guide and friend.

We pray that in this worship service
  we might feel your presence,
  feel you close.
We pray that we might open the doors of our hearts
  to your loving presence
  and know the joy you can bring.

Hear our prayer, O Spirit of God,
  and move in our lives.

Amen.

To Be Forgiven: Some Quiet Thoughts on the Love of God

"What Can We Really Believe?"
Theology in a Practical Key: Understanding Salvation (Soteriology)

Luke 15:11-32. I John 1:9: "If we confess our sins, he who is faithful and just will forgive us our sins and cleanse us from all unrighteousness.'"

God. Loves. You.

This is the most magnificent fact of human life.

Without deserving it, but so desperately needing it; without asking for it, though our souls secretly long for it; you and I are loved by the God of this universe with a love that beggars human description.

This amazing fact, the ultimate expressing of amazing grace, links our lives to the purposes of God and brings meaning into the chaotic wasteland of our existence. We can be God's children, and "If God be for us, who can be against us."

Too long has this dynamic, energizing, yes, **true** fact been shrouded in preacher-talk and smothered in stony tombs of churchly clichés.

We all know that God loves *humankind* — we've heard it from our childhood. But do you know that God loves **you**?

I'm afraid that you and I, like little Bobby Truex, have been to church so much, have heard the message of God's love so often, have become so familiar with religious thoughts, have fingered the sacred merchandise so long, that it has lost its mystery and we our sense of awe. And Bobby was only ten, a bright ten-year-old, in a Sunday school class my wife and I refereed many years back. I still remember well the class session when he delivered himself of a memorable summary of the life of Christ for his already-jaded peers: "We all know," said he, "how Jesus was born, and grew up, and never did nothing wrong, and healed

---

46

people, and taught people, and never did nothing wrong (this fact apparently impressed Bobby, and it should have!) and how Jesus died on the cross and rose from the grave and all that junk."

"All that junk." We adults sat bolt upright, wondering whether to be scandalized at some presumed sacrilege. But Bobby's classmates were unfazed. Bobby meant no harm, of course — the Gospel story, the story of the love of God for us, had become for him by the ripe old age of ten just a mass of meaningless verbiage. Or so he postured to his friends.

You and I might never be so blasphemous, or so honest, but many of us may well confess that the love of our God, offered in the Gospels as the chief dynamic of human life, is for us — practically speaking, just so much "junk."

Our tragedy is that we have been unable to accept this undeserved love, to live our lives in the responsible freedom that it brings. Why? Why is God's love to us still an abstract principle rather than a living reality shaping us every day? Why is it still in the category of pious talk, something to say to pass the time of day, religiously speaking? Why do we know it in our heads but not in our hearts?

I think one reason we cannot accept, or even understand, God's love is that our mental picture of God is not of one who is loving, lovely, or even trustworthy. From our relationship with our parents — especially our fathers — and with preachers and teachers, religious instruction, sermons, and popular representations of Christianity, many of us have constructed a picture of God who is something of a tyrant, a celestial traffic-cop, a whimsical, sky-bound bully who is looking over the ramparts of heaven to see if he can catch us when we err. A "gotcha" kind of God.

He represents authority. We are accustomed to rejection if we break the rules of authorities. We assume that when we break God's rules, God will reject us, too. Many of us are secretly afraid of God, would prefer that he leave us alone, not intrude, not mess around in our lives. For us, "God" equals "Fear."

Back when I was serving William Jewell College, I was driving from our town of Liberty to speak at a Wednesday night dinner at Wornall

Road Baptist Church in Kansas City, about fifteen miles away. I was running a little late and rushing, as we are all inclined to do, took the Broadway exit from I-35 a bit too fast, and suddenly was facing a large gentleman with a broad-brimmed hat and an innocent little radar gun held smugly in his hands. I was caught. And this, regrettably, was for me no trivial event, for I had been caught before at such nonsense, and I could lose my license if it happened one more time, and I couldn't do my job if I lost my license to drive — it is a privilege, you know, and not a right. So, after this traumatic encounter, and facing existing realities, I set about to correct things: (a) I put a Bible on my dashboard, (b) I hung on the rear-view mirror a little Buddhist prayer lantern "for protection against the police" sent by my son in Japan, (c) I bought a radar detector, and (d) I quit speeding. Not sure which of these worked, but something did. No more tickets.

It was a good dinner meeting at Wornall Road church, despite the painful interlude on the way, and I reflected on it afterwards — especially the unwelcome encounter with the distinguished officer of the law. Thought about it until it became for me a kind of life parable.

For you see, I had, for most of my life, looked on God just as I looked on that policeman. God was a great traffic cop in the sky, holding a giant spiritual radar gun, waiting to catch me and go "Zap!" and bust me real bad. Therefore, I had been living all my life with a spiritual fuzz buster on the dashboard of my heart, trying to avoid this threatening, frightening God.

"But No," said I in reflecting. "This is not God at all. This mental picture is of a bogus god, a fake, a phony, a bogeyman. The sooner I shed this picture for the true picture of God as revealed in the Bible, the better off I'll be."

When we cannot accept God's love because we feel unworthy of it, we miss the whole point. God doesn't *leave* us where guilt begins, where transgression occurs. It is precisely at this point that God's forgiving love *begins*.

God loves you. Period. End of story. It's not because you succeed in living the way your momma or your daddy told you that you ought to live, not because you are a good guy or gal or can convince God you will try to be, not because of your pedigree or other degrees, not because of your job title or your philanthropy or your dozens of good deeds. God loves you simply because God is God—God's character, God's nature is to love.

Hear the scriptures on this point:

> God commendeth his love toward us in that while we were yet sinners, Christ died for us (Romans 5:8).

> Herein is love, not that we loved God, but that he loved us, and sent his son to be the propitiation for our sin (I John 4:10).

> God so loved the world that he gave his only begotten son, that whosoever believeth in him should not perish but have everlasting life (John 3:16).

> God is love (I John 4:8).

Mr. Lansford, a counselor at McMain Junior High School in New Orleans, told me of a Mexican family who moved into his predominately Anglo neighborhood. An Anglo neighbor brought them a nice big cake as a welcome, and the Hispanic mother reciprocated by returning the cake platter filled with a delicious South-of-the-Border dessert. A couple of other hospitable exchanges ensued, and then one day Rafael, a lad of junior high school age, saw the Anglo neighbor's car in the drive and as an act of friendship took a pail and sponge and washed the car for his neighbor. That evening, there was a harsh knock on the door and Rafael's family was accosted by the angry neighbor man who told the lad in no uncertain terms that he wanted nothing done for him that he did not (a) ask for and (b) pay for. This angry response frightened and confused Rafael, and Mr. Lansford as his school counselor was helping him understand and accept.

It is clear, is it not, that the neighbor man needed to learn two lessons— first, the lesson of taking a young person seriously, and, second, the lesson *not only* of gracious *giving*, but also of gracious *receiving*. Even so, you and I may have two lessons to learn—first, the lesson of taking ourselves, and God, seriously in his love for us, and, second, the lesson of graciously *receiving* the loving forgiveness God offers, undeserved though it may be.

You see, God understands us, knows us, knows why we are what we are, why we do what we do. Knowing us, God has taken infinite pains for us in the person of Jesus Christ, so like the father in the parable, God receives us with open arms. My child was lost and is found. My child was dead and is alive again. Let us rejoice!

Because God understands us, God needs no explanations, no excuses from us. We are schooled at trying to justify ourselves when we have to explain our actions to our parents, or teachers, or husbands, or wives, or preachers. But God needs none of this.

When I was a village parson in Madden, Mississippi, I would sometimes "of a Saturday morning" cross the vacant lot by the parsonage and join the good old boys of that crossroads hamlet as they squatted in a circle on the red clay dirt out front of Gordon Chamblee's general store.

It was amazing how they could crouch there for hours, not quite sitting, not quite standing, but just there, knees bent, rocking on their heels, some of them chewing and spitting, some of them whittling, and the more talented ones chewing and spitting and whittling all at the same time. As the young "preacher man" up from seminary in New Orleans for the weekend, I was trying to be part of the "fellas" — you know, to sort of "connect." It didn't work. For one thing, I was half their age. For another, I didn't know much about raising cotton. For yet another, I never learned to squat like that. And still further, I didn't chew and spit and was a sorry whittler.

But mostly I couldn't "connect" because when I joined their circle everybody grew suddenly quiet. For a long time I was puzzled by this, maybe a bit offended, worried that maybe they just didn't like me, until finally one weekend a younger member of the group took me aside and explained it to me: they grew quiet because about 60% of their vocabulary was no longer available for use when the preacher was present. There were words, my friend said, that the preacher shouldn't hear, some of them no doubt words that no preacher had ever heard.

Then, after this awkward spell, as the men continued to chew and spit and whittle, it was always Lash Hardage, the *sort of* village reprobate (Madden wasn't big enough to have a *real* village reprobate), who broke the silence, and always with one of two questions: "How's things up at the church house, preacher?" (As if he cared.) Or, "Religion's in a sorry state in this little town, ain't it, preacher?" (As if he didn't know.)

Isn't it quaint, if not tragic, how we try the same childish tricks on God? We explain to God why we have failed or erred or sinned, we promise to do better, we offer a list of extenuating circumstances, we blame our parents for making us like we are, we blame our children (for as you know, insanity *is* hereditary—you *do* catch it from your children), we blame everything and everyone, sometimes including even ourselves. But this is foolish behavior. We can't trick God. We can't "explain away" things to God. God is God—and knows us. But more important, we don't *have* to play those games, for God is God—and loves us.

What do we do, then, to receive God's love, to find the forgiveness and healing and meaning that God promises his children?

We come to God just as we are, not armed with twenty new resolutions, not spouting promises to earn God's favor, but just as we are, warts and all, sins and all, problems and all. We bring all of what we are to God, and God loves and forgives and gives us strength to start afresh. For God. Loves. You.

Just look at today's text: the father in the parable did not ask for explanations or excuses. The son had made one up, to be sure—practiced his speech while walking down the road toward home: "Father, I have sinned against heaven and in thy sight and am no longer worthy to be called thy son. Make me as one of thy hired servants." See him, hear him, as he treads the dusty path, muttering, murmuring, practicing, "Father, I have sinned against heaven and in thy sight and am no longer worthy to be called thy son. Make me as one of thy hired servants." And he arrives home, and he begins, "Father, I have sinned against . . ." and his father interrupts him and throws his arms around him, hugs him, embraces him, kisses him, puts a ring on his finger and shoes on his feet, kills the fatted calf, says, "This my son was lost and is found, was dead and is alive again. Let us rejoice." No explanations needed. Just a father's love.

A mother wakes up in the night, hearing the cry of a sick child. She rushes to the bedside. Does she then insist that the child apologize for being sick, give explanations and excuses for getting sick, offer promises never to get sick again? No. The very thought is obscene. She rather tenders what help she can, ministering in her love to her little child.

When you and I call to God, from our sickness or despair or joy or just good sense, God understands and accepts us, for God loves us. "In my hand no price I bring, Simply to thy cross I cling." It is all very simple to say: we give all of ourselves that we know to all of God that we understand, and God accepts, receives, forgives, wipes away tears, makes better, makes whole. For God. Loves. You.

The young man sat on the porch of the beach cottage — Pensacola Beach, it was. He looked across the stretch of sugar-white sand to the blue-green sea, saw the waves ebbing and flowing, saw the sun slowing setting — and you have never seen the sun set, of course, until you've watched it on the sea. And he was thinking of the beauty of God's world, and the greatness of God's love that included even himself.

His reverie was interrupted by a car's arrival next door, then another, then another, and soon that bibulous American institution the cocktail party was in full swing. Drinks flowed, people grew noisier and more profane, and it was not long before someone sat down at an old out of tune upright piano and began banging out tunes. Popular songs, folk songs, and then — surprisingly — the strains of the little praise song about God, "He's Got the Whole World In His Hand." Laughter, cheers, jeers. Ah, this was all good, and raucous voices began to sing with the clangy piano — "He's got the whole world in his hand, he's got the whole wide world in his hand." Laughter, cheers, jeers. And more, "He's got you and me brother in his hand," laughter, cheers, jeers, "He's got you and me sister in his hand," laughter, cheers, jeers, "He's got the sinner man in his hand, he's got the teeny, tiny babe in his hands," laughter, cheers, jeers. "He's got the whole world in his hand."

And all the while the young man sat on his porch, gazing at the sand, and the sea, and the sun, feeling the wisp of a cool breeze across his cheek, feeling the silence and the softness, feeling caressed by all creation, and he mused, "Yes, indeed, God does have the whole world in his hand—not to laugh at, not for sport, not to jeer at, not even to cheer save in the holiest and most reverent of ways. He has the whole world in his hand, and he... loves... me."

It is true.

Our God does have the whole wide world in his hand.

And God. Loves. You.

Amen.

Pastoral Prayer

O thou God of love,

Hear us when we call to thee from our own far countries
Of loneliness
Of illness
Of grief
Of despair
Of guilt
Of need
Of conflict
Of anxiety
Of busy-ness
Of fear
Of failure
Or fear of failure.

Bring us to our senses.

Guide us back along the road to our Father's house,
Where we may find our true identity

not as hired servants,
not as pawns in cruel hands of destiny and fate,
but as sons serving
in responsible grown up freedom.

We confess that we have broken our relationship with you.
Bring us home, restore us this day, in your love.

Lord have mercy.
Christ have mercy.
Lord have mercy.

Amen.

Before the Benediction

In Australia, I am told, there once were many wolves and few sheep. Today, I am told, there are many sheep and few wolves. Do we conclude from this that the sheep killed the wolves?

Yes, we do.

For as the sheep gave themselves to the care of their shepherds, they were protected, cared for, their enemies destroyed.

Let us this week give ourselves to the care of our shepherd, who loves us. For God indeed loves you more than you can ever know.

Go in peace, then, to love and serve the Lord.

"9-1-1": How Do We Deal with Evil?

"What Can We Really Believe?"
Theology in a Practical Key: Understanding Discipleship

Micah 6:6-8. Micah 6:8: "And what does the Lord require of you but to do justice, and to love mercy, and to walk humbly with your God."

Tuesday, September 11, 2001. It feels like a long, long time ago. It feels like yesterday.

We have cleared the rubble and wreckage, but we have not cleared our heart's scars.

We have rebuilt, nobly and even magnificently — "the best response to terrorists," we say. But we have not brought back those who died.

We have fended off further attacks, but we have not quieted our fears.

We have watched the clouds of smoke and debris drift away, but we have not dispersed those close clouds of doubt that shroud our souls.

"9-1-1": a legacy of dread, a legacy of courage, a legacy of heroism, a legacy of resolve. And it is ours.

I am wondering what your thoughts may be today, your feelings, these several years out, after wars in Iraq and Afghanistan, after the rise of ISIS, after Ferguson and the anger and pain and violence that invades our streets, stalks our days, in all parts of America? Or after you have hurt someone terribly, or been hurt terribly? How does one stare into the face of evil and keep any kind of equilibrium?

I am not talking here of *explaining* evil, a question as old as the human race, never satisfactorily answered; I am talking of *living* in the presence of evil, going on despite it, dealing with it in a way that builds up life instead of tearing it down. This sermon series is, remember, *What Can We Really Believe? Theology in a Practical Key*, and so we look this morning not at the abstract issue theologians would call a *theodicy*, "the problem of evil," but rather at realistic, everyday discipleship—living with evil.

You and I face it in many forms, cannot in fact escape a kind of harsh badness that we begin to accept as "normal." The attack on the World Trade Towers is a dramatic example from our recent national history: we remember horrifying images of giant planes turned into lethal bombs, people leaping to their deaths, buildings imploding into mass graves, sirens screaming as heroic fire fighters and policemen plunge into a hell to pluck some out, tearful faces of wives and husbands and children, cries of the victims: "Help, help, help. O, dear God, please help me."

But at other times, it is a hospital bedside. I see my father lying there, tubes hopelessly giving nourishment and oxygen, nurses helping as much as they can, doctors rushing through with just a glance—for they know the score. Helpless he is, helpless am I as he cries out, over and over, on his way to death, "Help, help, help. O, dear God, please help me."

At still other times it is personal depression that gnaws away our spiritual innards; it is the anguish of harsh discord in a marriage; it is the pain of a child or loved one gone awry; it is the loss of work with its financial security and self-respect; it is the threats, the being violated, the being abused by urban ills like crime, violence, drugs, irresponsible greed and ruthlessness. And the cry is the same: "Help, help, help. O, dear God, please help me."

Evil stalks, war blasts, hate bites, sickness strikes, death calls, violence kills, and we want to *do* something. We want to charge against the enemy, right the wrong, correct the abuse, solve the problem. Some decisive action we want to take; but, alas, we can see no quick fixes, nothing that will make the evil go away overnight, or conquer it instantly, or resolve all dilemmas. How *do* we, then, deal with the evil in us, the evil around us? How *do* we deal with today's personal or global 9-1-1, and all of the 9-1-1's in our lives, at the moment of pain or in the extended pain of reflection?

For answer we turn to Holy Scripture and to our text of this morning: "And what does the Lord require of you but to do justice, and to love

---

56

mercy, and to walk humbly with your God." It may not be instant enough for us to feel quickly satisfied, but it is real enough for our walk with God to be ultimately satisfied. And it works. It *is*, in fact, how we deal with evil in our lives, how God's people have always dealt with the evil in themselves and the evil around them.

"**Do Justice [Justly]**," the text says. And it teaches us that in facing the huge wrongs, the dangers, the threats, the challenges of our day, we must first understand that **We Are Obliged. We Have Duty.**

This is not a popular word in our time, when the slogans are more like, "If it feels good, do it." "Go with the flow." "Whatever." "Just hang." But if we are to make a difference in this world, if evil is to be confronted and countered, if we are to build worthy lives, we have no choice — we must do justice. We are obliged. We have duty.

I might as well here confess to you my deprived childhood of growing up in a small-town Baptist parsonage, a household where there was an answer to every question, and it was "No," or "Don't." As kids, we weren't supposed to do anything, nothing; we weren't even supposed to *want* to do anything; man, we weren't even supposed to know about whatever it was we weren't supposed to do. So no drinking, no booze, for us. And no cigarettes — this before we knew it would kill you, back in the good old days when it was just a sin and not stupid, too. And no dancing. And no card playing with traditional playing cards, though you were allowed to play the card game of Rook with a Christian vengeance. And none of what they called "mixed bathing" — I think they meant swimming, and there is a difference. And no movies — after all, they were at the Cinema, as in "sin." Very, very negative it all was, with our Christianity defined in terms of things we should *not* do — little, even inconsequential things, it now seems, things that now have a kind of quaint and charming and nostalgic quality about them.

But, despite the seeming triviality of the issues, something very important was happening inside us, in our deepest souls. Some structure of character was being formed. We were learning that there is a Good, a Right to embrace and a Wrong to shun, that there are some things you do and some things you don't do. We are obliged. We have duty.

57

As we grew older, the issues became larger and much more important—feeding the hungry, resolving conflict, establishing justice in matters of race and sex and class, healing the sick, teaching and helping—and underneath these issues, still that spine of character saying, "We are obliged. We have duty. We do—justice." As Dr. Paul Bulger, my predecessor as principal of Harlaxton College in England, once said to me—using words he himself had read and stored up in his strong spirit—"If not us, then who; if not now, then when."

But there is more to the text. Not only are we to Do Justice; we are also to **Love Mercy**. That is to say, in facing the huge wrongs, the dangers, the threats, the challenges of our day, we must also understand that **We Are Flawed**. But, **We Have Love**.

How often have I claimed, have had to claim—everyday, really—that promise of I John 1:9: "If we confess our sins, he is faithful and just to forgive us our sins, and to cleanse us of all unrighteousness." Each of us is flawed. Each of us fails, falters, errs, strays from the path, sins against God and against others, especially those closest to us. And, bless God, despite these failings, each of us can be forgiven, cleansed, redeemed, and set on the road again to start fresh, to walk in newness of life.

As we are forgiven, so we are to be forgiving. We are to love mercy (translated also as "kindness," or "loving kindness" or "compassion"). We are to reach out to others with the forgiving love given to us by God. We who are flawed *receive* God's love, and we who are forgiven *give, offer, share* God's love.

Now, all of us can agree with these truths, bobbing our heads in unison at the obvious facts that we are to do justice and we are to love mercy. Yes, indeed. The trick comes in getting the two together, in a family, in a church, in a society, in a nation, in a world. How to blend justice—the rooting out of terrorists, making war against the current necessary enemy, executing murderers, or even such a maddeningly simple a thing as disciplining our own children—how do we blend "doing justice" with "loving mercy," at one and the same time?

When I was president of William Jewell College, some fraternity boys broke into the library in the dark night hours of finals week. My first response was an ironic one: "Good. They were so eager to get at the books to study that they just had to enter after hours." But it was all too apparent that they had been stealing final exams from a secretary's office, and the appeal of their suspension from school came eventually to my desk, as such cases inevitably did. Now I began to have help from all sides, all appealing that "this is a Christian college" and therefore a certain course of action was necessary. The faculty, generally, was saying, "Do justice. These young men have broken the central code of the academy, trying to graduate without doing their own work, stealing their way to a degree. This is a Christian college: therefore, do justice" (which roughly translated, as best I could tell, meant "kill them, or at least put them in stocks on the quad for public contempt"). But then I began hearing from mothers, and pastors, who were saying, "Love mercy. These boys have done wrong, but they are good boys, simply mistaken and misled. This is a Christian college: therefore, love mercy." How *do* you put the two together in complex, real-life situations?

Son Craig, when he was eighteen or so and a drama student at Jewell, was in trouble with me — again — and again was hearing my Speech #12, the one on measuring up to your responsibilities. (Craig either gave me many occasions to use this speech, or I am sad to say that I may have had an excessively quick Disciplinary Speech #12 trigger finger). We were on the sun porch of the president's home at the college, a place I used as a colorful and energizing little office, and I was getting into the speech pretty well, enjoying the sound of my own voice as I thundered justice and righteousness, my tones beginning to soar as I reached the climax of Speech #12, the one on measuring up to your responsibilities. Craig, I should say, simply stared at me at these times, never taking his eyes off mine — because if he did, of course, I would say, "Look at me when I'm talking to you, boy." And he never ever said a word in response because if he did, of course, I would debate his point and my speech would go on longer. And so I was just coming to a crescendo, the climactic moment of Speech #12, the one on measuring up to your responsibilities, when Craig did something he had never done before. He interrupted me! I was shocked, stunned, bewildered. This had never happened before, ever, in the history of our twain and shared worlds. And, in those moments of stunned silence what he said was, "You know, Dad, I have always enjoyed your performances."

Well, I lost it. I laughed, and laughed, and laughed, until finally I was able to say, "Baby, you have heard the last one; you will never hear another." And it was so. For son Craig was saying to me, in a charming and quite courageous way, that I needed to quit judging him for his faults and start letting him be, let him work things out in his own way. I needed not only to do justice, but also to love mercy.

"Do justice," says the text. And, "Love mercy." And, **"Walk humbly with thy God."** That is to say, in facing the huge wrongs, the dangers, the threats, the challenges of our day, in us and around us, we must also understand that **We Are His. We Have Life.**

> Do justice: We are obliged. We have duty.
> Love mercy: We are flawed. We have, and give, love.
> Walk humbly with thy God: We are his. We have life.

In the face of so much evil, such huge sin, such overwhelming hate, such threatening harm, how can society hold together? How can we be not overcome of evil, but overcome evil with good, as Scripture says? How can God's kingdom come, his will be done, on earth as it is in heaven?

I think that happens, ever so slowly, a little bit at a time, when we walk humbly with our God, each doing the work God gives us in the way God leads us in the time God allows us, Amen. There is no magic to it, no great manifestation, no breakthrough, seldom a newsworthy note, as "news" and "worthy" are judged by man. We simply walk with God, doing what good we can in the great world or the small. And our God does the rest. "Thy kingdom come, thy will be done, on earth as it is in heaven."

We celebrated Grandmother's last birthday thirty-five times. When she was seventy, someone in the family said, "Grandma won't be around much longer. We'd better get together and let her know we love her before she's gone." So we did. And she loved the party and came back the next year. And the next. And the next. She died one month short of her 105th birthday.

I gave a tribute to her at her church in Wichita, KS on her 100th (she was present!), telling the folks at that great Metropolitan Baptist Church that

---

I would be back on my 100th (I hope they remember, because I aim to show up), but mostly telling them that Grandmother was a bona fide saint—not because she was better than anyone else, but because she had outlived anyone who knew any dirt on her, which is the surest path to sainthood in this life.

In reflecting, though, and ironic jesting aside, I think she truly *was* a saint. For fifty years—fifty years—she looked after what they then called the "Cradle Roll" of the Kensington Avenue Baptist Church in the East Side neighborhood of Kansas City. Can you imagine how many gallons of milk or juice she hauled to church in fifty years, how many pounds, tons, of cookies, ginger snap or chocolate chip, made never with a recipe but with a dash of this and pinch of that and dab of the other and smidgen of these, world class cookies made perfect every time—and I was a connoisseur who knew. Can you imagine how many diapers of future ministers she changed in fifty years, how many noses of future deacons she wiped, how many tears of future teachers and missionaries she dried? How many persons she spoke to, as she walked the streets of her neighborhood—she never learned to drive, and it was safe back then to walk—telling mothers and fathers that God loved their little baby and God loved them, too.

Grandmother's name was never in the newspaper; she was never called a great Christian; she was never "on TV for Jesus." Nobody would have ranked Cora Evalena Edith Stone Payne with the great leaders of the church. But for fifty years this good woman did what God had given her to do. And I can't help but think that her rewards were greater than those of us who talk a lot but haven't been so faithful. She faced the evils of her world, of her own soul—and in more than a century of life there were many evils, including two world wars on the outside, and who knows how many roiling struggles on the inside—by walking humbly with her God.

Do you understand? We walk humbly with our God, and as we do so God does God's work.

He takes the little bits of good that you do and links them with the bits of good that I do, and the good that she does, and the good that he does, and the good that they do, and this combined good falls on God's earth like drops of rain, refreshing the earth, forming themselves into little rivulets of good that become a stream that become a river that become finally a great, great ocean of God's goodness and God's love.

> O the deep, deep love of Jesus,
> Vast, unmeasured, boundless, free!
> Rolling as a might ocean
> In its fullness over me!
>
> Underneath me, all around me,
> Is the current of Thy love
> Leading onward, leading homeward
> To Thy glorious rest above!

The sheer magnitude of this good overcomes the fierce, pointed shards of evil, overwhelming evil with the accumulation of good wrought by God's people.

It is all very simple. Not easy, but simple. How do we deal with evil? How do we go on? As the Lord requires, we do justice, we love mercy, and we walk humbly with our God. And God does the rest.

In the name of our Lord Jesus Christ,

Amen.

Pastoral Prayer

O Lord save us.
O Lord make us free.
O Lord preserve us in the midst of evil around us,
And from the churning evil within us.

May be do justly, may we love mercy, may we walk humbly with you,
That your kingdom may come,
That your will may be done,
On earth as it is in heaven.

Amen.

"What a Piece of Work Is Man!"

"What Can We Really Believe?"
Theology in a Practical Key: Understanding Humankind (Anthropology)

Psalm 8. Psalm 8:3-5: "When I look at your heavens, the work of your fingers, the moon and the stars that you have established; what are human beings that you are mindful of them, mortals that you care for them? Yet you have made them but little less than God, and crowned them with glory and honor."

> What a piece of work is man! How noble in reason! How infinite in faculties! In form and moving, how express and admirable! In action how like an angel! In apprehension, how like a god! The beauty of the world! The paragon of animals!

So speaks Hamlet, Prince of Denmark, in one of Western literature's great flights of praise toward humankind—we saw this play at the Royal Shakespeare Theatre in Stratford-upon-Avon on the very day America was attacked by terrorists. And that timing made it very credible to hear the next words of troubled, despairing Hamlet:

> And yet, to me, what is this quintessence of dust? Man delights not me; no, nor woman neither . . . (Act II, Scene 2).

William Shakespeare, through his Hamlet, voices the height and the depth, the soaring and the sinking, the ecstasy and the agony of being human. In this, he mirrors our days. And so we bring The Bard to our aid as we continue this sermon series on *What Can We Really Believe? Theology in a Practical Key.*

Don't you have times when you feel so good you can't stand it, when you feel you can take on the world and win, when you can climb mountains and cross oceans and fly like winged victory through all the skies of the universe. Nothing can stop you. No one can defeat you. And so like Cyrano de Bergerac, who has just heard Roxanne speak her love to him and feels he can triumph over any foe, you trumpet, "Bring me giants!"

"What a piece of work is man! . . . "noble . . . infinite . . . admirable . . . like a god!"

But don't you also have days when you are looking up to see bottom, when you are so defeated, depressed, despairing that nothing is right, nothing is good, there is no hope, no health, no happiness to be found?

Then you feel like "quintessence of dust" and intone, "Man delights not me; no, nor woman neither . . . . "!

Shakespeare's words presage not only our personal but also our cultural sense of ourselves. Through all our Western history men and women have seen themselves in the way Shakespeare, and our Psalm 8 text for today, describe us: "What a piece of work," "noble," or as the Psalmist says, "but little less than God, crowned with glory and honor." We are capable of great good and great bad; we achieve great deeds; we commit great wrong; *and we are responsible for each.* In the end of all, we can take ourselves to destruction, or we can be redeemed, can be "saved." It is the way the Bible, the Judeo-Christian tradition, the Western historical-literary tradition describe us.

But in more recent decades, this understanding of humankind has taken its lumps, with dire consequences. Whole dissertations could be written on this, and in fact I once perpetrated one of them, to my lifelong dismay. But in the simple caricature allowed by a twenty-minute sermon, it goes something like this:

"Modern" thinkers describe for us a traumatic loss of our identity as special creations of God, unique and responsible and noble.

Popular readings of Darwin make us victims of biological forces beyond our control.

Popular readings of Marx make us victims of economic forces beyond our control.

Popular readings of Freud make us victims of psychosexual forces beyond our control.

And in popular readings of Nietzsche, the whole game of a special relationship with God is lost in Nietzsche's announcement that God is dead. (Though I can't help remembering, and enjoying, the two banners—really hand-lettered sheets—hanging from adjoining dormitory windows at Wake Forest University, one reading, "God Is Dead, signed, Nietzsche," and the next reading, "Nietzsche is Dead, signed, God.")

The net results have been two: (a) first, a rampant "anything goes" mentality, a relativism telling us that anyone's values and beliefs are as valid as anyone else's, so it pretty much doesn't matter what you do—a kind of theological and moral free-for-all, that is; and, (b) second, a terrible diminishment of the stature of humankind.

No longer are we Robinson Crusoe, heroically creating a world of order and purpose on our desert island Earth; instead we become Robinson Crucifieds, buffeted, bawling, brawling, braying, whining victims who sit in the middle of our island circle, lament our lot, and blame any and all and every—blame God, blame the universe, blame our parents, blame the people around us, blame anyone but ourselves. We have become, in nineteenth, twentieth, and now twenty-first century writings, Hamlet's "quintessence of dust." "Man delights not me: no, nor woman neither . . . . "

Our writers say it for us, and I could offer dozens of quotations from modern classics.

Eugene O'Neill, in his autobiographical play *Long Day's Journey Into Night*—just listen to the title—penned, "None of us can help the things life has done to us." Victim words, the literary and psychic badge of our time. "I am not responsible."

Tennessee Williams has his character Big Daddy say, in the play *Cat on a Hot Tin Roof,* "Man is a beast that dies. The human machine ain't no different from the fish machine, or the bird machine, or the reptile machine. Man is a beast that dies."

T. S. Eliot's poem, so characteristic of a modern malaise, chants,

We are the hollow men
We are the stuffed men
Leaning together
Headpiece filled with straw. Alas! . . .

This is the way the world ends
This is the way the world ends
This is the way the world ends
Not with a bang but a whimper.

It is a root sickness of our times and our lives, this diminishment of humankind.

The common theme in this incantation of loss is the word *victim*. And what a swelling Victim Chorus we hear every day of our lives, in office and club and media and street. Sometimes even, in our attempts to be helpful, we encourage and intensify the victim feeling among recipients of our efforts.

To be sure, there *are* legitimate victims in this world—victims of war and flood, fire and disaster, abuse and neglect. The Gospel is clear about our duties to such people, and one of the great good things of our Western society is the effort, at every level, to help those in genuine need.

But, honestly now, don't you get tired of hearing folks whining when their lives are really quite good, their opportunities even better, yet who are determined to see themselves as sufferers? There they are, all around us—they *could* act as responsible, capable, even noble men or women, but instead they lower themselves to whine, and to blame, and to whimper.

Not to be trivial, but take the guy who sued McDonalds's, Burger King, Wendy's, and Kentucky Fried Chicken because he is overweight. Not that I would prejudge any person, and I will gladly take instruction from some of the many astute lawyers in this congregation, but c'mon now—didn't the guy buy the fat burgers himself and shovel them into his fat belly all by his little lonesome? And he's a *victim*?

Or try something like, "My broker lost money for me so I'm suing him." Hey, who took the risk, eyes dancing all the while in hope of obscene gains at the other end?

Or try, "The government is to blame because the roads and bridges are bad—stupid government," but in the next breath, "No way will I vote or pay a tax for roads and bridges."

Or, "Our schools have failed us totally," without a word about how little children are sent up to the schoolhouse who have never held a book, never been held in someone's arms while a story was being read, little children who are looking this way and that to avoid being beat up or shot—and it's our *schools* that have failed us? C'mon, now.

At an unnamed place where I once worked, a colleague whined for a week about some weeds outside an entrance door, complaining loudly about the grounds maintenance staff, going on at length about inept people and a bad work ethic and uncaring supervisors and cheapskate management. "How do they expect us to do a good job in our own work when they won't even keep the place up in a decent way?" Then it happened that we walked in to work together one morning, and I asked her to show me the weeds. They were three in number—count 'em, three—and it took less than eight seconds to pull them up. But it was so much more satisfying for her to be a whining, complaining victim than simply to lean over and yank the blasted weeds. This experience, I submit to you, is a modern-day parable.

Even more tiring, though, than hearing other folks whine—after all, any of us can be a social critic and condemn what others do—is our feeling like victims ourselves, whining ourselves, inside our own heads or to others.

We all do it now and again, maybe because our culture has seeped into our own bones so we feel we must talk like victims, or maybe because we sometimes really *are* victims of chance or injustice or tragedy, or maybe because we just like to vent. But when our victim-ness (our littleness, our pettiness, our fearfulness, our complaints, our laments) becomes our defining sense of who we are, we have lost something very precious, indeed—the ability to see ourselves as God sees us, and to act in responsible and heroic ways.

Psalm 8 defines it all for us:

> When I look at your heavens, the work of your fingers, the moon and the stars that you have established; what are human beings that you are mindful of them, mortals that you care for them? Yet you have made them but little less than God, and crowned them with glory and honor."

Our God describes us in regal terms, sets us right up there as a centerpiece of all creation.

Let us, then, believe God, and believe God's word. I don't mean to be simplistic, and I know something of the intricate path we must take toward healing when psychiatrists and psychologists are helping us. But surely if we say in our heads, then begin to feel in our hearts, that we are special to God, that we are in fact "but little less than God," that we are "crowned with glory and honor" by God, that we can indeed be responsible and worthy and even noble, it will affect the way we walk through this world. We can be, indeed we are, God's own children, and as the Holy Book tells us, "If God be for us, who can be against us."

We can even force a dialogue between our Self and our Soul:

> If our Self says, "My parents messed me up,"
> our Soul can answer, *"But I am responsible for what I will become, and I am 'but little less than God.'"*

> If our Self says, "I am not loved,"
> our Soul can answer, *"But I am responsible for what I will become, and I who am 'but little less than God' am loved by God."*

> If our Self says, "My work situation is bad, or my work doesn't mean anything,"
> our Soul can answer, *"But I am responsible for what I will become, and I am 'but little less than God,' and God has very important work for me to do, if I will just break out of my self-centeredness and help someone else."*

> If our Self says, "I'm not able to measure up," or "I have no luck in life," or "I fail, I fall from the right path," our Soul can answer, *"But in God's eyes, I am responsible for what I will become, and in God's eyes, I am 'but little less than God.'"*

"What are human beings that you are mindful of them, mortals that you care for them?" the Psalmist asks. And the answer comes, "But little less than God. But little less than God."

How long *can* a four-year-old girl in seat 16F of Aer Lingus Flight 125 from Dublin to Chicago stand in that seat talking to the bald-headed man in seat 17G behind? The answer is 7½ hours, non stop, with

"What's your name?" moving to

"How old are you?" ("Older than you.") and then to

"Your hair is funny — there's none on top."

But it was all worth it, for her next question was,

"Are we bigger than the sky?"

"No, we are not bigger than the sky."

"Yes we are. See? [*She points out the airplane window.*] We're up here, and it's down there."

Yes, children, children of God, we are bigger than the sky. "But little less than God," we are, and "crowned with glory and honor" in the eyes of our God.

Leslie Weatherhead, when he was pastor of London's historic City Temple, wrote a charming tale of a father and his little boy out walking in the English countryside, as English people like to do. The father and son were passing from one village to the next, villages so close the church steeples were in sight of each other, when a soft autumn shower caught them. Taking refuge under a huge chestnut tree until the shower had passed, they were delighted, as the sun came out again, to see a beautiful rainbow arcing across the sky and settling softly in the misty green valley below.

The little boy grew so excited he raced pell mell down the hill, hoping to find the end of the rainbow and the pot of gold that would surely be there. But alas, he was sorely disappointed, for once having arrived, he found no pot of gold at all and, in fact, could no longer even see the rainbow as he looked around himself. His father, however, on the eminence above, saw his little son at the bottom of the gentle green slope all bathed, clothed, in the soft colors of God's beautiful rainbow-promise, God's glorious rainbow-gift. And the father was joyful to the point of tears.

You and I feel our pain, our weakness, our hurt, our failings, our disappointments, and they are real enough. But there is more to us than that, and God sees all that "more," all that "good." God has shaped us, found us worthy of love, redeemed us in Jesus Christ, walks with us day by day, will care for us forever. So God looks on us from his divine hilltop, sees our frustration and puzzlement, but sees us also bathed, clothed in the rainbow colors of his promised love and forgiveness and grace.

God knows us as we really are, and, behold, it is very good.

In the name of our Lord Jesus Christ,

Amen.

Pastoral Prayer

O God,
We feel so frail, so vulnerable, so exposed.
Sometimes, often, we are afraid.

Things don't go right.
There is tension in our marriage.
Our children fail us, as we fail them.
Our parents ask for more than is possible.
We are laid off from work, or wish we could find a way to leave
    bad work.
We grow old.
We grow ill.
We don't know what to do, where to turn.

And some things are so big, God,
    that we can't understand them,
    and certainly can't do anything about them.
We fear terrorists but can't see them.
We fear nuclear and biological weapons but can't control them.
We fear rogue states and demonic leaders but can't touch them.
We care for those who suffer from others' greed
    without knowing how to quench that greed.
We care for those who suffer from cataclysmic events
    without knowing how to stop those plagues

like famine or homelessness or epidemics of disease
from breaking out.

We feel so small.
We throw ourselves on the mercy of your divine court, knowing
that this Judge loves us with an infinite love.

Lead us through the various valleys of our various shadows of
our various deaths, and bring us out again in fullness of life.

Strengthen us so we are strong when things don't go right, so
we learn from our failures and disappointments.

Lift us up so that whatever happens around us we may trust in
you and fear not.

Thank you for making us as we are,
"but little less than God,"
"crowned with glory and honor."

May we feel this nobility, this grand stature, in our lives this
day.

In the name of our Lord Jesus Christ,

Amen

"When the Roll Is Called Up Yonder"

"What Can We Really Believe?"
Theology in a Practical Key: Understanding the Future (Eschatology)

John 14:1-7. John 14:1 "Do not let your hearts be troubled. Believe in God, believe also in me."

"So," our son Aaron asked me, as he was standing at the stove in our kitchen, stirring a pan of a gloppy something-out-of-a-box called "Tuna Helper," the presumption apparently being that canned tuna can be helped. "So," the young man asked, "do you think Darrel Porter went to heaven or hell? I mean, like, he was a good man, but he died, like, of a cocaine overdose?" More stirring in the pan. Then, the first question still suspended somewhere in tuna fumes above the stovetop, "When do you think the world will end? I mean, like, we are having the floods and wars and all that stuff the Bible talks about." Still more stirring. And then he wolfed down the whole platter of that gloppy something called "Tuna Helper," along with a small steak and after that some leftover hamburger concoction, and questions of the afterlife seemed less urgent to him.

They are big questions to ask, though, especially over a pan of Tuna Helper, and they echo the curiosity, the concern of men and women for centuries. "What will happen next in *this* world?" "What will happen in the *next* world?" "*Is* there a next world?" "Will the world end, and if so will it be by some kind of fiery holocaust, and will it be soon?" "What happens when we die?" "What is heaven, and will I go there?" — this one is asked with a hopeful eye. "What is hell, and am I in danger?" — this one is asked with a grimace, a shudder, as if fearing somebody might know something.

We all think we would like to know the future — we probably wouldn't, really — so that we might find some sense of — well, if not control, then at least hope. It is scary out there, in that unknown glacial distance beyond us. If we only knew what was going to happen. And if we were only sure that it would all be good, that everything would be all right.

It has always been so. In Bible times people were as curious as we are, and so when teaching Jesus refers often to ideas of heaven and hell and eternal life, all the while teaching us how to live right now right here on earth. His disciples, however, want specifics on what comes tomorrow — they are less enthusiastic about what they should be doing today — so they ask things like who gets to sit on the right hand and who on the left in the big-shot big-time kingdom, and when will things start cranking their way anyhow, until Jesus has to tell them in some exasperation, "It is not for you to know the times or the seasons, which the Father hath put in his own power" (Acts 1:7).

Not to be left out, St. Paul gets into it all by assuring the Thessalonian Christians in quite vivid, movie-scene-like descriptions that "the Lord himself shall descend from heaven with a shout, with the voice of the archangel, and with the trump of God: and the dead in Christ shall rise first" — the graves apparently giving up their consignments as gruesomely as in a painting by Hieronymous Bosch, "then we which are alive and remain shall be caught up together with them in the clouds, to meet the Lord in the air: and so shall we ever be with the Lord." (This in I Thessalonians 4:16-17 — notice that Paul is expecting this Second Coming of Christ to happen while he is still alive. This first letter to the church at Thessalonica is probably the first written book in the New Testament, dating from about 52 ad, less than twenty years after Jesus's death, and so St. Paul expects things to be happening fast!)

When we get to the Book of Revelation, we are into a "new heavens and a new earth," with a heavenly city described in specific detail — streets are paved with gold, for example; it is 12,000 furlongs (1,500 miles) around the city walls; the walls have twelve gates, and so on. Hell, on the other hand, is a lake of fire where the worm is quenched not, there are various beasts to contend with, and all in all it is not a happy place. This Book of Revelation is, to be sure, highly symbolic writing in a literary form called "apocalyptic" — a conquered people using fanciful, extreme images with hidden meanings their captors couldn't understand — the Book of Daniel in the Old Testament is another example. But it has been taken in literal, intense earnestness by centuries of popular, folk Christianity.

And so Dante, in the great epic poem of the Middle Ages, writes what is called *The Divine Comedy* — comedy not because it is funny but because it turns out well — in which he as literary character goes through all the levels of hell and purgatory as a sort of spiritual tourist before finding bliss in heaven, with God and Jesus and even his allegorical childhood sweetheart Beatrice. John Milton, in *Paradise Lost*, likewise gives exciting descriptions of Satan and hell as part of his effort "to justify the ways of God to man." These popular images of the afterlife, of heaven and hell, are dominant ones in our literature, so important they are in our collective consciousness. (When I was examined for the ministry by an ordaining council in Florida, in fact, a very astute pastor asked me if our mental images of hell come mostly from the Bible or from John Milton; "John Milton" is no doubt the correct answer.)

On an even more popular level, these word pictures are writ large in our religious music, especially that of oppressed or struggling peoples — as in our Negro spirituals or the rousing Gospel songs of the frontier. Here there is a hope of heaven, of a better life on the other side, mixed with an occasional hint of Christian revenge — you sorry guys have had it good here, but just wait 'til over there. So,

> I got a robe, you got a robe,
> All o' God's chillun got a robe.
> When I get to Heaven gonna put on my robe,
> Gonna shout all over God's Heaven,
> Heaven, Heaven,
> Ev'rybody talkin' 'bout Heaven ain't goin' there,
> Heaven, Heaven,
> Gonna shout all over God's Heaven.

Or, "Deep river, my home is over Jordan"; or "There'll be peace in the valley for me"; or "There is a balm in Gilead to heal the sin-sick soul"; or "Lord, I want to be in that number/When the saints go marchin' in."

> On Jordan's stormy banks I stand
> And cast a wishful eye
> To Canaan's fair and happy land
> Where my possessions lie . . . .
> I am bound for the promised land . . . .
> Oh who will come and go with me,
> I am bound for the promised land.

"When all my labors and trials are o'er/And I am safe on that beautiful shore . . ./That will be glory for me" — my ninety-seven year old mother wanted that sung at her funeral. And it was. "Ring the Bells of Heaven," "Shall We Gather at the River," "There's a Land That Is Fairer than Day," We're Marching to Zion," "'When We All Get to Heaven," and of course,

> When the trumpet of the Lord shall sound,
> And time shall be no more,
> And the morning breaks, eternal, bright, and fair;
> When the saved of earth shall gather over on the other shore,
> And the roll is called up yonder, I'll be there.

The hope is real. The yearning is real. The hunger to know, to understand what lies ahead — that is real, too.

And so, a whole religious industry has grown up around that desire to know what comes next. I have read the books, seen the charts. We are offered, by people who mean well but couldn't have a clue, detailed descriptions of the geography of heaven and hell, specific timelines on what comes next — wars and rumors of wars, earthquakes, floods, then the second coming of Christ in the sky, the so-called "Rapture" when the saints — Christians — are caught up into the heavens, then seven years of a great tribulation on earth when "The Beast" is unchained, then the Judgment Seat of Christ, and the Second Coming of Christ and his saints to earth to defeat Satan and to rule for a thousand years of peace and plenty, then the Great White Throne of the Last Judgment when the damned are sent to eternal hell and the saved to eternal bliss.

In my impressionable early adolescence — you won't believe this but it is true — having heard these images and fears and hopes from assorted energetic, even athletic preachers, I came home from school one evening to find lights on in our house, the radio playing, and no one around. I was both puzzled and worried, and so I scurried over to the church next door, where I found lights on in the parlor, a gas fire in the grate, chairs in a circle, but no people. Where could my family be? Where were all these good Christians who were supposed to be at this meeting? I was terrified, so sure I was that Jesus had returned, the Rapture had occurred, all true believers had been snatched away to heaven, and here I was left among the damned. And deserving it. It is quaint and humorous and even charming to look back on it now; but then, I felt real terror.

These over-zealous efforts to explain what cannot be explained are unfortunately wrong-headed, of course, however well intentioned they may be. In their zeal to explain what can't be known, these preachers grab a verse of scripture here, a patch of a text there, a hint of an idea up here, a Biblical image down there, and weave them into supposed truth, as if it were dictated by God and were now as somberly factual as an article in Encyclopedia Britannica—or, heaven bless us, even in Wikipedia. And then these same preachers thump Bibles and pulpits up and down the land "explaining the future" to intrigued, often frightened hearers—chief fright being felt by impressionable kids as was I. Yet Christ's teaching remains, "It is not for [us] to know the times or the seasons, which the Father hath put in his own power"— Jesus said that to his disciples in Jerusalem *then*, and he says it to us in Kansas City *now*.

I know we would like to have inside information on what comes next, what it is like after death, what heaven is or hell or judgment. It is our nature to want to know. Robert Browning said it: "A man's reach should exceed his grasp/Or what's a heaven for?" Or William Blake: "Less than everything cannot satisfy man."

But I have to tell you, as a person who spent eleven years in formal college and theological study and a lifetime reading the Bible and thinking about these things; I have to tell you as a person who wears these robes as the preacher, the authority figure, the minister of this morning; I have to tell you as the person standing behind this pulpit, this sacred desk, holding my well-read Bible, this sacred book—surely the religious buck stops here if it stops anywhere; I have to tell you that on these questions of eschatology, of "last things," *I simply do not know*. That's the long and the short of it—*I don't know*. That's pretty poor, I recognize, for this sermon on eschatology, on last things, in this series on *What Can We Really Believe? Theology in a Practical Key.*

Should I, then, take these ministerial robes off, as an ineffective enlisted man has his stripes ripped off his sleeve by his superior officer? I guess I should, in all honesty. In fact, I think I will. [*Robe is removed.*] And I stand before you in shirtsleeves not as "Reverend," not as "Senior

---

76

Minister," not as "Doctor" Kingsley, not claiming or offering any special wisdom from my hard-earned ThD, my Doctor of Theology degree, but rather as a fellow seeker, one making this *Pilgrim's Progress* with you as John Bunyan wrote it, going *"from this World to that which is to come,"* through the Slough of Despond, the Valley of Humiliation, the Valley of the Shadow of Death, Vanity Fair, and the Delectable Mountains, all on the journey to God's Celestial City.

Let me not pontificate, then, but just share with you, not as preacher or theologian but as fellow pilgrim making the journey, walking our common road. Let me share with you how I deal with these "last things" like heaven and hell and judgment, the end of the world and the afterlife, how they make sense for me. If this sharing, this testimony, makes sense for you and helps you, well and good. I'll be very glad. If it is sort of empty to you, then I can give you a list of "real preachers" who may be able to help you better, or at least will claim to know more about these "last things" than do I.

So.

In my own heart and mind, I deal with heaven and hell and the end of the world and judgment and the afterlife first by saying I can do nothing about them then, out there, but only here and now. These things are in God's hands, not my hands. And if I am not doing what I can do for God, being what I can be for God, believing God right here and right now, then at the point of death or judgment or heaven or hell it will be way too late to worry about it. So I concentrate on now. (Jesus himself in fact taught this, that the kingdom of God is "at hand," is "in you," that we are to walk with our God day by day, hand in hand, doing God's work by serving others in the here and now.)

I believe that God is just. We can't trick God or fool God or slip around God. A true and faithful recompense comes to us for our thoughts and deeds, the things we commit and the things we omit. We experience some of God's justice here, now. It is at least reasonable to presume that we may experience it in another sphere, another zone of our souls. For God is just.

I believe that God is love. As we walk with God, God forgives us our sins, God wraps us in his love and grace, and we become God's child—

now, and for eternity. Nothing, nothing, nothing can separate us from the love of God—now, and for eternity.

I believe in eternal life as Jesus taught it. It does have some connotation of longevity in it, numbers of years, quantity of time, "life everlasting." As the country-Christian song says, "Got so many million years I cain't count 'em." But Jesus's primary meaning was *quality* of life—how we use the time and the life God has given us, here and now, on this earth.

For myself, I must let others speculate on the rivers of clear water that flow from the throne of God in the new Jerusalem; what I need to do is offer my little cup of cool water to the thirsty person at the sides of the roads I walk right now, bread to the hungry ones, a touch of healing to the sick ones, a word of care to the ones hurting.

The only way I know how to deal with eternity is to deal with the present; the only way I know to live with angels and avoid demons is to live with real people in their real life joys and to fight real and present evil every day.

I believe the future is in God's hands, and I trust God, and I am content.

"But what happens when we die?" we frantically ask.
"I don't know, and I don't need to know."

"But when will the world end, and how will it come?"
"I don't know, and I don't need to know."

"But what is heaven like—or hell?"
"I don't know, and I don't need to know."

Let not your heart be troubled: you believe in God, believe also in me. In my Father's house are many mansions: if it were not so, I would have told you. I go to prepare a place for you. And if I go and prepare a place for you, I will come again, and receive you unto myself; that where I am, there you may be also.

And whither I go ye know, and the way you know. . . . I am the way, the truth, and the life . . . (John 14:1-6).

"Let not your heart be troubled."

You and I make our lives today, and God takes care of tomorrow.

Last things are interesting.

But first things are first.

In the name of our Lord Jesus Christ, who will see us home,

Amen.

Pastoral Prayer

Dear God,

We feel very much this morning like people of the road, pilgrims on a
   steep journey, hoping to catch sight of some promised land beyond.

Give us hope, we pray,

But mostly give us endurance,
and a sense of direction,
and a strong staff to hold us up,
and bread to feed us,
and water to nourish us,
That we may make our way.

We understand, in our deepest selves, that the journey is not about the
   arriving, but about the going,
That the purpose of the pilgrim is to be a pilgrim.

So guide us, Lord, and walk with us.

As some of us grow sick on the way, help and heal us.
As some of us lose loved ones, comfort us.
As some of us stray from the path, bring us back.

As some of us falter, strengthen us.
And sometimes, let us rest, and drink cool water, and sing some songs, and pray some prayers, and feel the presence of good people around us.

Maybe these gifts may be ours this morning, Lord, in these moments of worship, as we wait upon you to show us the way.

Even so we pray, with all our hearts.

Amen

"The Communion of Saints"

Ephesians 4:4-6, I Corinthians 10:16-17. I Corinthians 10:17 ". . . we who are many are one body."

Bethlehem. Picture it in your mind. A white frame church, at the crest of a hill, in open country near Harrisburg, MO., a village itself not far from Columbia.   The church was founded in 1821, the same year Missouri became a state, in the house of one Fielding Wilhoite.   The white frame building came not long after.

Out front, under giant oak trees, is a rolling lawn and a large stone block with steps carved in it—used in past years for dismounting from wagons or horses.   Though most folks drive pickups to church, Roy Rummans sometimes rides his horse, his wife Fannie having died in the last year, and he uses the stone platform and steps as did his father and his grandfather before him, even ties his patient horse to an iron ring set in the block.

Out to the side—north, I think—is the church cemetery, where generations of folks with the same names as those now living lie "in hope of resurrection": Trimbles and Thurstons, and Hills and Burks and Crenshaws. We "decorate" the graves once a year, on Memorial Day, though at other times you may see small bunches of flowers left by family members who have come "back home" for a visit. Men of the church keep the cemetery mowed.

It is October, 1956, and I, a graduate student at the University of Missouri, am the new pastor of Bethlehem Baptist Church—for such is its name—my first charge as a terribly young and green minister. I work diligently on my sermons, which are nevertheless terrible: they are dogmatic, shallow, glib, narrow—I still have copies of some of them, and they are continuing lessons in embarrassment and humility. The church pays me $25 a week, and it is way too much. I don't realize all this, of course—I knew a lot more in 1956 than I know now. Fortunately, I don't hurt many people with my earnest but clumsy

---

81

preaching, for only twenty-five souls or so show up on a good Sunday, and that includes Jess Trimble, who sits over by the pot-bellied stove in winter, or cools himself with the funeral home fan in summer, and goes to sleep every sermon I preach. Every one. I finally work up the courage to ask him, "Jess, why do you go to sleep during every sermon I preach?" And he chuckles and says, "I got a lot of confidence in you, boy, and I need the nap; besides, I'm seventy-five years old, and no twenty-one year old has much to tell me." I am offended, of course; but of course he is right.

The old folks tell me of the good old days at the church, how they would have revival meetings second week of August, after crops were laid by, and people would come from miles around and would fill the whole spacious building, how folks would even stand outside the windows in the summer nights and listen to the preaching and singing, 'cause there wasn't any room inside the church. That was before folks started moving to town, you know. We decide — well, really, I decide, and they go along with it — to have a "homecoming," as they call it, celebrating Bethlehem's 135th anniversary. Folks do come "home" from all over the nation; amazing it is. I invite my dad up from Florida to preach, and many friends from his former large-church pastorate in Columbia come out to see him, hear him. We fill the church — first time in decades. I send two little boys out to stand by open windows and look in and listen, and I say to Jess, "See, it's just like it used to be." And his eyes fill with tears, and he brushes them away real fast.

During the "Homecoming" service, folks stand up to give what they call "testimonies" about what the church has meant to them; and a middle-aged man who has driven with his family all the way from Washington, DC, to be at that homecoming, an air traffic controller fellow, stands and sort of shuffles and sort of speaks in a kind of stumbling way, concluding, "'bout the only thing I know to say is this: it seems to me the kids who grew up in this church are still going to church." And he sat down, having said it all.

Clarence and Edgar Burks are so proud, Mrs. H. H. Thurston is so happy, Eddie and Buelah Hill smile, as does old Roy Rummans through his ancient watery eyes. And Jess Trimble even stays awake for this service.

You see, these heroic folks were keeping a ministry alive, keeping a witness for Christ alive at Bethlehem, a church that began on the rough frontier, a church that knew glory in the days when Missouri was her farms, a church that declined as Missouri became towns and cities and folks moved away. They didn't know they were heroes, of course. They were just coming to church — showing up Sunday by Sunday, teaching, praying, singing, giving, helping their neighbors, telling them Jesus loved them.

And the kids who grew up in that church — seems like they are still going to church.

The good people of Bethlehem wouldn't ever even have heard the words from The Apostles' Creed, printed on the front of your bulletin for today, but they were living it out — something about a "communion of saints." Bethlehem Church is gone now, but that "communion" lives on for those of us who drank from her simple well of faith and love.

Notre Dame, Paris. Now make a very large shift in the picture in your mind. To the beautiful boulevards of Paris and to the glory of Paris, Notre Dame Cathedral. The Roman Catholic "Cathedral of Our Lady," is its proper name. It is Sunday, March 10, 2002; my Protestant wife Suzanne, our Protestant missionary friend Kim Newell, and your obedient humble and Protestant servant are attending the ten o'clock mass in this great church of Christendom, begun in 1163 and 122 years in the building — still today, 1,000 years later, a center of vital worship.

It is a magnificent building, as beautiful in its way as this one where we worship today: stone sculpting centuries old, exquisite wood carvings, mystical stained glass windows, arches and spires reaching upward into the darkness where God must surely live (or so the peasants thought in the Middle Ages), the great organ swelling its sounds to fill all the massive space, giant metal-studded wooden doors protecting the body of Christ from centuries of marauders without, even crazy gargoyles carrying away rain water while scaring little kids and other demons.

This particular liturgy is sung and in Latin, a mass in Gregorian chant. My pitiful two years of high school Latin unlock few mysteries of this liturgy to me, nevertheless I know what is being said. I can tell it from

---

the cadences, from the placement in the service: "Our Father, who art in heaven, hallowed be thy name, Thy kingdom come, Thy will be done, on earth as it is in heaven"; or, "I believe in God, the Father almighty, maker of heaven and earth; and in Jesus Christ his only Son our Lord. . . I believe in the Holy Ghost, the holy catholic Church, the communion of saints, the forgiveness of sins, the resurrection of the body, and the life everlasting, Amen."

The sermon is not in Latin but in French, and my pitiful two years of college French unlock few mysteries of this quite passionate sermon, nevertheless I understand that we are "voir avec les yeux de la foi" — to see with the eyes of faith. "Once I was blind, but now I see," is the Biblical text. I take communion at the altar, trusting my Catholic friends will forgive me this breach of their theological etiquette, though of course not a soul there knows who I am or what I believe, save for Suzanne and Kim. Being French and therefore "cool," most of the persons present couldn't care less what I do, and those who do care will surely understand that my soul wishes, yearns, to feast spiritually on the bread and wine, Christ's body and blood, the life of our Lord. Bien!

And magically, mysteriously, across barriers of language, and customs, and denominations, and centuries, and orthodoxies, there is wholeness. We are one with our French brothers and sisters, Catholics they, Protestants we, praying, and singing, and giving, and knowing, "one holy catholic [the word means 'universal'] church," knowing indeed the "communion of saints."

St. Columba's, Glencolmcille. Now, please, shift your mental picture once again, away from the busy streets of Paris to a village in the remote west of Ireland. The church is St. Columba's, Glencolmcille, County Donegal, Ireland—a tiny stone church, a bit run down though the few communicants work hard at keeping the place up, a church which sits at the head of the beautiful glen on the very spot where St. Colmcille established his tiny monastery in the year 545 or so. It is now a Protestant church, "Church of Ireland" it is called, in an utterly, wildly beautiful setting—the surrounding mountains clad in bracken and heather; the Glen Head cliffs jutting out into the Atlantic; the sea rolling or crashing against sheer stone faces; deep, mysterious mists and fogs presiding over all at this centuries-old place of worship.

It is July 14, 2002. Usually wife Suzanne and I, for this is our "church home" when we are at our little cottage in Ireland, arrive at noon, the stated time for the service to begin, and people are just then beginning to show up. Things are casual in Ireland. Our presence swells the attendance from ten to twelve souls, all of us listening to Mamie Maxwell play the old pump organ—she wears her teeth on Sunday, but not during the rest of the week, all of us listening to the peppy vicar Rev. Gordon Freeman try to stir up an unstirrable flock, all of us listening to pillar-of-the-church Anne King read the lessons from the Bible—always it is Anne King who reads the lessons, always—most surely, in the Glen, Protestant children grow up thinking the whole Bible is Anne King reading, the "Gospel According to Anne."

But this day is different. At eight minutes to noon there are already twelve cars outside, along with two Massey Ferguson tractors. Something special is clearly happening. And it is—Francis Simon and Patrick Lawrence are being baptized, and their adoptive mother Anna has invited godparents and family and special friends, some coming all the way from England, one even in a green kilt. This is special.

To the baptismal font go the two boys and the minister. In this liturgy of baptism they renounce Satan, evil powers, and all sinful desires; they embrace Jesus Christ as Savior and Lord, "putting their whole trust in his grace and love"; Rev. Freeman thanks God for the gift of water and reads the baptismal words—"I baptize you in the Name of the Father, and of the Son, and of the Holy Spirit. Amen. We receive you into the household of God, the communion of saints"; and he baptizes Francis and Patrick by pouring water thrice over their heads—in the name of Father, Son, and Holy Ghost. It is beautiful, a holy time, a ritual old as Christianity.

But this is no ordinary baptism of ordinary Irish children. For these are Francis Simon and Patrick Lawrence Ossulu, and they are from Africa, and these "infants" are ten and eleven years of age—quite good soccer players, it is said, quite good additions to the Glencolmcille school team—and their adoptive Irish mother Anna has saved them from certain death by starvation or war in their home village, has given them a new home and a new life, and now they begin a new life in Christ.

Later in the service, Francis and Patrick take up the offering, in a certain non-Irish, lively style — actually, they are juking down the aisle as Mamie Maxwell, teeth and all, makes that organ rock. And still later, I kneel with them at the rail to receive communion, and as I rise from my knees, though it is not my place to do so, I unobtrusively and momentarily lay my hand on the bowed head of each African-Irish lad as he kneels at the rail, silently offering my blessing and receiving theirs in return. And in that moment for me, across continents, across cultures, across languages, across customs — I feel the communion of saints.

Country Club Christian Church. Which brings us to this day in Kansas City, at beautiful Country Club Christian Church. I must tell you the effect this place has on me. I had not been inside this edifice, except for Lisa Brown and Tom Van Saghi's wedding, until I first stood to preach here, last February. I had never before heard the music of this place, experienced the powerful integration of song and word and prayer and fellowship that constitutes worship in this very special house of worship.

When I first stood in this pulpit, I was like the young Martin Luther celebrating his first mass in May of 1507 — I could scarcely continue, it was all so powerful, so awesome, so moving. Even still, when I drive up early on a Sunday morning, and look at this place, I say, "How is it that I would be so privileged as to minister here. Thank you, God."

And the blessings have continued. I shall not soon forget the children singing "Whatta Buncha Lunch" or lighting candles as acolytes; David Diebold and Dale Ramsey at two organs, here and in the balcony; the magnificent music week by week, offered by so many people; communion led by your Elders; the embrace of all races, all churches, all people, in this place and in this community; the dedication of this church staff and lay leadership; the beauty of this house of God; the array of ministries as people go out from the church to make a difference in our world. What a great church is here on Ward Parkway in Kansas City!

And this church is doing precisely the things that have been done at Bethlehem on that rural Missouri hilltop, or Notre Dame in Paris, or St. Columba's in Glencolmcille, Ireland — worship, fellowship, prayer, preaching, study, evangelism, missions, helping those who need our help. It is a communion of saints.

The church of our Lord Jesus Christ is one. That church is holy. That church is catholic, that is to say, universal. Therefore I do believe, as do you, in "one holy catholic church."

And this "communion of saints," this "one holy catholic church," is your place and mine; and it is Jess Trimble's waking or sleeping at Bethlehem; and it is Pere Joseph-Marie Velinde's as he presides over mass at Notre Dame; and Patrick and Francis Ossulu's in Glencolmcille; and St. Colmcille's himself in the fifth century, in the same place; and Martin Luther's in the sixteenth century. We are all one. We share in this great communion of saints, across centuries and across continents. For, indeed, "the ground is wondrous level at the foot of the Cross."

Because of this church, this body of Christ, this communion of saints, you and I are never alone. We are never weak unto death. We are never without support, never without love, never without grace, never without hope. We have not only the God above us, the Christ before us, the Holy Spirit within us, but all the church, the body of Christ, around us and with us.

I urge you this morning: open yourself to this miracle. Make yourself a part of it, and it a part of you.

In the name of our Lord Jesus Christ, head of his body the church,

Amen.

Pastoral Prayer

We need you, Lord,
And we need each other, too.
And so we thank you for this "communion of saints" called the church.

We thank you for people who care, who even care for us.
We thank you for their attention, their comfort, when we are sick.
We thank you for their support, their care, when we are in grief, or
    difficulty, or sorrow, or despair, or defeat, or confusion.

We thank you for the influence of your church in our cities, feeding the
    hungry, caring for the homeless and helpless, attending to those in
    nursing homes or prisons or hospitals, offering "communion" to
    those who so earnestly need "communion."

We thank you for the power of your church in our world, as an
    influence for peace, for compassion, for understanding, for health
    and wholeness.

We thank you for church schools and colleges, for church care for the
    elderly, for church care for children, for church hospitals, for
    missions and evangelism, for church buildings and church
    programs, for the ministry of presence such as this on Ward
    Parkway in Kansas City.

But chiefly we thank you for the communion of saints,
across all ages and all times and all generations,
across all countries and all languages and all cultures,
across all denominations and creeds,
across all prejudices and narrowness.
Thank you that we belong — to you, and to your church — and that our
    lives are thereby saved.

In Jesus name,
Amen.

"The Body of Christ"

"What Can We Really Believe?
Theology in a Practical Key: Understanding the Church (Ecclesiology)

I Corinthians 12:12-27. I Corinthians 12:27 "Now you are the body of Christ and individually members of it."

The Apostle Paul, in a remarkable section of his first letter to the Christians at Corinth, tries to explain to these unruly brothers and sisters, who are suffering from a nearly terminal individualism and self-indulgence, what it really means to be part of the church of our Lord Jesus Christ.

What a crowd, these Corinthians: arrogant, quarrelsome squabblers they were, vying for positions of power in the congregation, doing the "he said, she said" kind of thing, hurting each other in trying to become #1. Ever see that in a church? Factions, and faction fighting?

They were boastful. There was serious sexual immorality among them "of a kind that is not found even among pagans," said Paul. They were suing each other in the secular courts. They were gluttonous and getting drunk at the church dinner preceding the Lord's Supper. They were disorderly in their worship. They were behaving in ways that made people wonder what kind of religion they had, what kind of god they were serving. They were bringing shame on the followers of "The Way, the then-name for the new Christian religion. And finally Paul, in exasperation, summarizes, "Fornicators, idolaters, adulterers, male prostitutes, sodomites, thieves, the greedy, drunkards, revilers, robbers — none of these will inherit the kingdom of God" (I Corinthians 6:9-10). Not exactly a model congregation!

And to these people St. Paul said, "Snap out of it. Shape up. Get a life. Get real." (I know that's not the exact language of the Bible, but that's what he meant.) "Church life is not every man for himself. It's not what can I get out of this. Instead — "Now get this," he says, using a word picture even our youngest children in Sunday school or Vacation Bible School could understand — ("Read my lips," he says) — instead, it's this way:

89

"As the church, Jesus is our head."

And, "As the church, we are the body of Christ—one, harmonious body."

Listen to Paul's exact words:

> Now you are the body of Christ and individually members of [one another] . . . . If the foot would say, "Because I am not a hand, I do not belong to the body," that would not make it any less a part of the body. And if the ear would say, "Because I am not an eye, I do not belong to the body," that would not make it any less a part of the body . . . As it is, there are [many parts], many members, yet one body. The eye cannot say to the hand, "I have no need of you," nor again the head to the feet, "I have no need of you." . . . If one member suffers, all suffer together with it; if one member is honored, all rejoice together with it . . . . You are the body of Christ.

A simple, clear word picture this, straight out of Holy Scripture. "Now get this." "Read my lips." A child can understand.

Ever since Paul wrote these words, "body of Christ" has been one of the main descriptions of who we are as the people of God, as the church. There are other names: *ecclesia*, or "gathering" (the same word as *synagogue*); "chosen generation"; "royal priesthood"; "new Israel"; "family of God"; and others. But no image has been more enduring, more compelling, more clear than "body of Christ."

What does it mean? Practically speaking—and we *are* trying to be practical in this sermon series on *What Can We Really Believe? Theology in a Practical Key*, as today we take a further look at the doctrine of the church, or ecclesiology. Practically speaking, for us this morning, sitting on these cushy pews in this beautiful church on elegant Ward Parkway in eminently livable Kansas City, what does "body of Christ" mean?

As we put our names on the Friendship Register and so, I guess, sign on in some way; as we say the Lord's Payer; as we sing the hymns, or don't; as we share in the bread and wine of communion; as we endure yet another sermon—what is this image "body of Christ" saying to us?

At least two major things, I think.

I. First, that **we are God's action agents in this world.** Christ is the head; we are the body. Christ leads; we work.

A general has to have troops on the field of battle. A coach has to have players; a choral director has to have a choir; a conductor an orchestra; a dramatist a cast; a CEO a company; a law firm partners; a hospital doctors and nurses and technicians; a teacher a class. When we think of a head without a body it is grotesque, bizarre, even frightening, like in a science fiction or horror movie. Someone indeed has to lead.

When I was in college work, stories would go around a sort of circuit from school to school, often becoming the most entertaining and educational part of a professional gathering. I guess that is true in any business or profession or trade. In any case, I was charmed at one such meeting by a story out of Smith College in Northampton, Massachusetts, a tale which may have even been true. The college, so it went, had sent out a questionnaire to parents of entering students that included the query, "Is your daughter a good leader?" And a father filled in the stunningly honest answer, "No, but she is a good follower." This dad received a personal phone call from the president, congratulating him on his daughter's admission to the college and adding, "With 3,000 good leaders in the student body here at Smith, we need at least one good follower."

Even so: We are good followers. We serve our Lord and we meet human needs by *following* the head of our church, Jesus Christ, who directs us as we do what we call "the work of the Lord." That's why New Testament descriptions of life in the church are short, decisive action words: "Go." "Teach." "Make disciples." "Pray." "Preach." "Give." "Be ye doers of the word, and not hearers only, deceiving your own selves" (James 1:22). In Biblical terms, we are all ministers – for we are the body of Christ. Christ our head cannot do his work in the world without us.

The Deacons and Elders of this congregation, serving communion each Sunday, are to me a powerful symbol of this truth:

Christ our head is symbolized here in the bread and wine on the communion table;

then, the hands and feet of our Deacons and Elders, their eyes and hearts, move up and down these aisles, in and out among these pews, *serving* us — we who are the body of Christ.

You and I take these sacred elements with our fingers, our hands; they go past our lips, onto our tongues, into our bodies — and we not only symbolically receive, but symbolically *are* the body of Christ.

And these same hands and feet and eyes and hearts and bodies go into the community to serve day by day.

So, one Elder prays at this table for our "commitment to live a life of compassion for all of your people, of love for all of your creation, and of mercy for all the downtrodden. Amen." Another Elder prays, "Show us ways that we can respond and serve." And together, we are the body of Christ, doing God's work.

There is a legend — and it is just a legend, of course — that Jesus returned to heaven at his Ascension and was met by a chorus of angels singing praises to him as Son of God. A spokesangel stepped from the choir to ask the question on all angel hearts: "Good Master, is your work on earth completed?"

"My work of redemption is accomplished," said our Lord, "but my larger work on earth is just beginning."

Murmurs of dismay through all the heavenly host, and the spokesangel asked, "But Good Master, whom have you left to do your work on earth?"

"A few fishermen, some peasant women, a tax collector, a radical revolutionary or two, a handful of others."

More murmurs of astonishment and a great fretfulness before the obvious question, "But Good Master, what if they should fail?"

To which our Lord responded quite simply,

"They cannot fail. They must not fail."

Our hands are the only ones our Lord has to reach out to others in care, our minds the only minds to think God's thoughts after him, ours the only lips to speak and sing God's praise, our feet the only feet to carry God's goodness to others, our hearts the only hearts to share the beat of divine love.

We are the body of Christ.

We cannot fail. We must not fail.

II. The second thing the image "body of Christ" teaches us is that **we belong to each other, we are part of each other, we need each other, we *are* each other**. "Now you are the body of Christ," Paul wrote, "and individually members of [one another]."

Ezekiel 37 is a wonderfully dramatic passage in the Old Testament, parallel to our New Testament text of today, in which the prophet sees the dry bones in the valley first connected to each other, then covered with flesh, then filled with breath (spirit), and then come alive again.

As the Negro spiritual sings it, "the foot bone connected to the ankle bone, the ankle bone connected to the leg bone, the leg bone connected to the knee bone, the knee bone connected to the thigh bone, the thigh bone connected to the hip bone, now hear the word of the Lord." We are connected. We are connected.

We need each other; we have each other; we *are* each other — the body of Christ.

The airplane lands at Dallas/Fort Worth airport — American Airlines Flight 1119 — and I am on it. The chime sounds, the light goes off, seat belts click open, people leap up into the aisles, and then what happens? Instantly, cell phones fly out, numbers are punched in, and then sentences like, "Hello, we've landed"; and "Hi, I'm at DFW Airport now. Hope to catch an earlier flight to Austin"; and "I'm here. Are you in the parking lot?"

I stand there in the aisle, feeling sort of left out, sort of not with it. I wish for a little fake plastic phone so I can pretend I'm calling someone, though I really have no need to call anyone, and if I did there is no one who cares that I'm in DFW airport and hoping to catch an earlier flight to Austin. So why do people do this needless nonsense?

Ah, it's all very clear and very simple. They want to feel connected. Connected. Somehow, somewhere, they are not going it alone. They are connected to other people, people who care that they have landed, that they are going to Austin, that they need a ride home.

Even so. The body of Christ. We are connected. We are caring for one another. We matter to one another — where we are going, what we are doing, whether or not we get "home."

T. S. Eliot wrote it, in his poem *Choruses from "The Rock"*:

What life have you if you have not life together?
There is no life that is not in community. . . .
Even the anchorite [the hermit] who meditates alone . . .
Prays for the Church, the Body of Christ incarnate.

St. Paul also wrote it, as you have heard: "If the foot would say, 'Because I am not a hand, I do not belong to the body,' that would not make it any less a part of the body. And if the ear would say, 'Because I am not an eye, I do not belong to the body,' that would not make it any less a part of the body . . . . You are the body of Christ and individually members of [one another]." We are one.

His name is Rich. He is standing, this night, at one end of the great altar in Grace and Holy Trinity Cathedral downtown, part of a circle we had formed around this large table of God, with its giant candlesticks pointing toward the heavens, its Holy Book open, its sacred wine-filled chalice standing sentinel next to holy bread. We are a group who know each other, for we are sharing in a concluding Eucharist, a true communion, after a year of every-Tuesday-night study as new communicants in the Episcopal Church.

Rich had struggled through this year of classes, because the catechumenate was essentially a set of verbal exercises, and it is hard for Rich to talk. His ready smile and pleasant face become contorted when he tries to speak. He labors at it. He stammers. He forms his lips carefully and places his tongue willfully and still the words don't come. The simplest sentence is a major battle and uttering it a major triumph.

94

And so here we are, standing in the circle around the great altar, at the climax of the communion service, sharing with one another those symbols of the body and blood of Christ. It begins with the minister, the priest, who first offers the bread to the person next to her, saying, "The body of Christ, the bread of heaven." And on around the circle it goes, from hand to hand, from hand to lips, each time for each person with the murmured words, "The body of Christ, the bread of heaven." Close behind the bread will be the cup, offered by each person to his or her neighbor with the words, "The blood of Christ, the cup of salvation." We are sharing the sacred meal of the body of Christ.

And the bread comes to Rich. Sandra offers it to him, saying quietly, "The body of Christ, the bread of heaven." And he takes the bread in his hand, and places it on his tongue, and takes it into himself. Then he turns to Michael, places the bread in Michael's cupped hands, and struggles to say to his brother, "The body of Christ, the bread of-" "But it won't come. His face twists. He strains, turning his tongue, pursing his lips, trying to get the phrase out, "The body of Christ, the bread of—," The body of Christ, the bread—, " "The body—, " "The-the-bread—," and it will not come. Beads of sweat form on his brow. Tears well up in his clear blue eyes.

We all stand in the circle waiting, praying for him, reaching out to him with our spirits, making the words silently with our own lips, trying to help him. Again and again Rich tries, again and again he fails, until finally, on maybe the thirty-somethingth try, he gets it out: "The body of Christ, the bread of—heaven." "Heaven," he says, and in joy and relief repeats it again and again, "Heaven, heaven, heaven, heaven, heaven." And he sits down, spent, exhausted, silently weeping."

Michael takes the bread into his mouth and into his being, and we take that bread and that moment into our hearts—and, with one voice, we break the sacred stillness and cheer. Cheer. Applaud. Right there at the communion table, the altar of God. We thank Rich, and we thank God for this expression of faith that triumphs over all our human limitations. And we can't help it. We look at each other, we look at Rich, we look at each other again. And then, together, we sort of chant in unison, clapping it out for Rich, and for ourselves: "Heaven, Heaven, Heaven, Heaven, Heaven." And his smile is from sea to sea, star to star, face to face, heart to heart. So are ours.

Is this not what the Christian faith is all about? Is this not what the body of Christ is all about? When William Sloan Coffin was chaplain at Yale, a student challenged him in a public meeting by parroting a line from Communist dogma, "Christianity is just a crutch." Dr. Coffin thought about that for what seemed a long while before replying, "Indeed, Christianity is a crutch. But who's not limping?"

We need each other. And, bless God, we have each other. The body of Christ. The nourishing bread of Heaven. Of Heaven. Of Heaven. Of Heaven. Of Heaven.

In the name of our Lord Jesus Christ,

Amen

.

Pastoral Prayer

Dear God,

We thank you that we are joined with one another as the Body of
    Christ.
We need each other, to be at our best in serving you.
Most certainly, we need you.

And so we ask for help.
Some of us feel, in our private selves, that we have tried to go it alone
    for so long, and we are weary.
We have been disappointed in others, and we have disappointed
    others.
We have been hurt, even as we have created hurt.
It is hard for us to trust, to believe, even to hope.
And so we turn into ourselves, isolating ourselves, cutting ourselves off
    from others, making ourselves to be alone, sometimes, even, quite
    lonely.

Help us in this day to know your love, to *feel* your love, so we can have
    courage to open our hearts.

Please, dear God, break through our walls, our shields, our shells, our
   fortresses, our defenses.
Wrap us in the warmth and comfort of who you are. Teach us who we
   can become.
Help us to rest in your love and in the love of one another. Help us to
   be a whole and healthy part of the body of Christ.

We pray not just for ourselves, selfish though we be. Cure, clear away
   our selfishness.
We pray for those who need our help, and we pray that we may follow
   our prayers by becoming those who help.
We pray for those who are sick.
We pray for those who grieve.
We pray for those who are hungry, helpless, homeless.
We pray for leaders of this world, those with authority and
   responsibility, especially as our own leaders make momentous
   decisions of war and peace.
We pray that we may be good stewards of the goodness of this earth,
   recycling, renewing, preserving, saving.
We pray that we may be good stewards of our lives.

Dear God,
We need you, and we need each other.
And so we ask for help.

Amen.

Belief Matters

"What Can We Really Believe?"
Theology in a Practical Key: A Life with God

I Timothy 4:6-16. Mark 9:23-24: "Jesus said to him, 'If thou canst believe, all things are possible to him that believeth.' And straightway the father of the child cried out, and said with tears, "Lord, I believe; help thou mine unbelief."

It does matter, you know, what we believe.

Sometimes we'd like to pretend that it doesn't. We do so want to get along with others, almost at any cost, and our beliefs can divide us. "Two things I won't talk about—politics and religion," a common refrain.

And so, trying to get along in pluralistic America—and we spread the circle ever wider as the pluralism grows, so that we are now way beyond just Baptists and Methodists and Disciples; way beyond just reaching out to those people of strange liturgies called Episcopalians or Catholics; way beyond, even, reaching out to our Jewish brothers and sisters; we are now talking of Muslims and mosques, Buddhists and temples, and many more, mostly Asian religions—trying to get along, we start mouthing quaint little sayings like, "It doesn't matter much what we believe: we are all just in different boats headed for the same shore." Well, maybe. But probably it would do us well to check out both ship and shore, if we are going to bank our lives on them.

Or we say things like, "If we just follow the golden rule, we'll all come out okay." God knows it will help us to follow the golden rule, but there must be more to life and faith, than that!

I recently had lunch with my professor son in the crowded faculty dining room at Georgia Tech, and that busy scene put me in mind of a tale I had read earlier:

At one of the great Eastern universities, in a similarly crowded faculty refectory, a professor of theology from the divinity school chances to sit at table with a professor of astronomy from the science faculty — it

---

98

being the only seat available. They introduce themselves, and the astronomy professor is bemused at meeting the first theologian he has ever talked to in his entire life. He can't help himself — everyone fancies himself a theologian, you know — and so he blurts out what he considers a profound comment: "I'm not much into theology, I have to admit, but I get along. You know my theology? 'Do unto others as you would have others do unto you.' That's my theology."

The theologian ponders that one for only an instant before she responds somewhat in kind: "Well, I'm not much into astronomy, either, I have to admit, but I get along, too. You know my astronomy? 'Twinkle, twinkle little star, how I wonder what you are.' That's my astronomy."

Bingo. As a theologian, she was right on the mark. If we are to live a worthy and rich and full life, certainly a Christian life, we must go deeper than our friendly feelings, deeper than bland little comments like "all in different boats" or "do unto others" and get to some substance, some strength, some fiber, some content, some meaning in our personal belief system, in our personal theology, which leads us directly to our personal walk with God.

Why? Because what we believe determines what we do. Because what we believe shapes who we are. I still remember when a journalist defined and derailed a candidate's run for the Presidency by writing, "He's a good man, but down deep, he's shallow." If down deep we are shallow in our theology, in what we believe, we will live shallow lives, and we will be shallow persons. No one wants that.

So, today we conclude our twelve-sermon series on *What Can We Really Believe? Theology in a Practical Key* by considering why our theology matters and how it becomes a winsome, vital, living faith, a life of love and trust in relationship with a living Lord. Now, don't even think about getting bored. For this is where your life is at, at its core, whether you know it or not.

Why is our theology, our personal belief system, important?

Ask Mohammed Atta, in the pilot's seat of American Airlines Flight 011, Boston to Los Angeles, as he turns the plane toward New York and the north World Trade Tower. "Why do you do this, Mohammed Atta?

Why are you ringleader in a terrorist plot that will kill more than 3,000 people this day, that will scar the most generous and open people the world has known, that will take your own life? Why, Why, Why?" And you hear the answer: "I believe in an Allah of vengeance. I believe that America and Americans are evil. I am destroying evil. I do this because of what I believe, because of my theology."

Ask the suicide bomber who straps explosives around her body and goes into a crowded restaurant. Ask the accounting chief at a corporation that "cooks its books" so it can cheat its customers. Ask the brother who gives up his kidney so his sister can have a transplant. Ask Mother Teresa, ask the finest man or woman you know, ask yourself. And it is abundantly clear: what you believe shapes how you act, determines who you are.

Our beliefs are the steel girders, the superstructure of our life's building; our feelings are the dancing fountain out front. Our beliefs are the bread, the meat and potatoes and vegetables of the banquet of life; our feelings are the fluffy soufflé dessert. Our beliefs are the bedrock we stand on; our feelings are the shifting sands of everyday events. That is why a firm grasp of our God — our grasp of God, and God's grasp of us — is so very important. This becomes theological and spiritual *terra firma*, a place to stand where most things bob adrift.

Our beliefs, then, are important. And so **how do we form a worthy theology, a system of beliefs which leads us directly into a deeply satisfying life of strong character, buoyant hopes, and an everyday walk of goodness and love?**

First I need to offer the caution that it is not in the way we often think, the way we often hear it, from a lot of TV and megachurch preachers, and if truth be told from the voice inside ourselves that wants everything to be easy and simple. Our faith is much too important, much too life-shaping, for us to pluck some slogans off a TV screen or church "stage" and call it our theology.

There is a whole sweep of American religion and politics now rampant in the land that offers simple answers to complex questions, does it noisily and angrily, and demands that everyone else agree. These messages often come to us in slick media packages, "selling" a partic-

---

100

ular brand of theology as effectively as the ubiquitous TV commercials sell the latest miracle drugs. And, lacking a religious "Food and Drug Administration," this religious media bombardment isn't even required to include those soft-voiced, rushed narrations at the end of the commercial telling you how this drug can hurt you, even kill you.

But we simply must not settle for slogans and sound bytes, for simple solutions and easy, glib answers that may make dramatic points, may claim to be "right," may give us clever and dramatic words to say when the topic of religion comes up, but do not calm the ache in our souls or give us a worthy purpose for our lives. Down deep, it's . shallow.

I bear personal witness: I grew up as a fundamentalist Christian and at sixteen or seventeen years of age thought I knew most of the answers to most of life's questions. Then life happened. And I needed something else, something much deeper. I wasn't noisy about it, didn't make a scene about it, but I was quietly searching.

My family and church friends would say, "Just believe the simple Gospel, like we believe." And I did and I do believe the Gospel. And I tried to believe it quite simply, like they believed it. But I just couldn't make myself say that people who had never even heard of Jesus Christ would "burn in Hell for eternity." Or that every single word of the Bible was literally dictated by God himself (I believe the Bible, very much so, but that is another matter entirely). Or that only Christian people can know the God of the whole universe. And on and on and on.

When I took my questions to my preacher-father, who loved me, his very powerful theological answer was, "I don't want any of your smart mouth." And later, as president of a Baptist-related college, I would from time to time be bludgeoned by some fundamentalist pastor who suspected that I did not, or that members of my college did not, hew to his literalistic, fundamentalistic, angry brand of faith.

In this time of search, I was helped by a friend, later lost through an untimely death in a small-plane crash, a man with the improbable name of Grady Nutt. Some of you, of my generation, may have seen him on an old television program called *Hee-Haw*. He was a Baptist minister as well as a gifted humorist. Grady would tell me, and others, of visiting church folks as a pastor in rural Kentucky with two Bibles in his possession, a giant hardback model in his hand and a little New Testament in his shirt pocket. The giant tome he called his "Dog Bible," for as Grady told it, the houses in that part of rural America were set up on concrete blocks, and under every house or porch would be a skinny, mangy, snarling, malnourished dog who seemed to love preacher-meat and who would therefore lie in wait for preachers to come, at which moment it would race out barking and growling and threatening imminent dismemberment or death. Grady would wait 'til just the right moment, then would pop that dog smack on the snout with his giant Dog Bible, at which point the mangy dog would get religion and go whining, scurrying back to his lair, while the preacher would go on up to the house to try to help the folks inside, reading to them out of his little pocket New Testament.

I think Grady was trying to tell me, in his winsome way, that we can be growled at and snapped at, we can be the objects of noise and anger, but we need to keep right on going with the Gospel in our hands — and in our hearts. I think Grady was trying to tell me that God doesn't promise us that our lives will be always simple, our paths always easy; instead, God promises to walk with us through the complexities and the difficulties.

So Grady helped me. Other friends helped me. Listening to the wisdom of the church helped me. Reading the Bible helped me. Thinking things through, then thinking them through again — that helped me. Having a growing experience of God in my life helped me. And as you can see, we are back to the first sermon in this series, on how we can know God and God's truth. From this complex set of actions and experiences, I myself, and thousands, millions of others, have found their "theology," their core beliefs that lead them to a daily walk with God in security and harmony and in doing what is good — "the next right thing."

I know it all sounds very complex, which is why the theological slogans and strident assertions that "I am right" are so appealing to any of us, to all of us. But if we look at it not in terms of dogmas or slogans but in terms of a relationship, a loving relationship with a loving God, then the complexity disappears. Instead, it becomes as simple as a little child's reaching with her small hand, feeling her father's large and strong hand enclosing hers, and the two walking together into whatever lies ahead.

To repeat it for emphasis, so we can be sure to "get it": creating our personal beliefs is not just a saying "Yes" to some simple slogans, though that is often a starting point, especially for young children. "Believing" is not a willful, mechanical act, nor is it some kind of force-feeding through Jesus-y or Bible-y tubes, or a repeating of what a preacher or teacher or pamphlet tells us to say. As a revered teacher of mine once said, "The simple Gospel is not as simple as simple people like to think."

Instead, finding our theology, shaping our beliefs, finding what makes sense to us and makes our lives more rich and full and holy—all this is more like forming a deep love than it is like signing a card that says, "I agree. I believe what you say."

How does it happen that you grow to love someone? You learn who they are. You hear their story. You learn where they have been, where they are going, what they yearn to become. You like what you hear, what you see. You are drawn to it all, drawn to that flesh and blood, that vital living person. He or she becomes in some ways, many ways, "Beautiful." At the same time, the same thing is happening for them: he learns who you are. She hears your story. She learns where you have been, where you want to go with your life. He shares maybe a similar history, similar life goals. He or she is drawn to you.

That is to say, your two life stories come together as one. They first connect, then they intersect, then they intertwine, and—if it becomes a real love, your stories combine. Your story becomes his story, her story becomes your story, you begin to live one and the same story.

A worthy theology, a worthy structure of beliefs, comes in much the same way, I think. As little Ernest, in Nathaniel Hawthorne's "The Great Stone Face," kept looking at the noble features of the great carving on the mountain until those features became his own, so we link our story, our life, with the life of God until we take on something of "the face of God," Godly ways of thinking and behaving. When we love someone, are close to someone, link our lives with someone's, we

---

103

begin to think alike, we begin to speak the same phrases, do the same things. So with God. Our relationship with our Lord becomes the substance, the content, of our personal theology, our beliefs.

To be sure, there come times when we need to translate that love, those beliefs, to rational statements in the form of language, for clarity and discipline, and so we can tell others and even focus ourselves. And here books and learning and the expressions of others can help. But the substance, the root "theology," comes from that loving relationship with our Lord.

We don't sing the song much anymore, but with all its sweetness it has tough truth. It goes, "Tell me the old, old story of unseen things above,/ Of Jesus and his glory, of Jesus and his love." This is not only solid theology; the hymn also reminds us that Bible truth is *story* truth. God's truth is *story* truth. The *story* of our need, the *story* of God's grace, the *story* of God's strength, the *story* of God's forgiving love. It is the *story* of a prodigal who comes home, the *story* of a man left for dead at the side of the road until a good Samaritan "binds up his wounds," the *story* of a Jesus Christ, son of God, who would die as an expression of his love for us.

You look at that story, you are drawn to that story — that God loves you, cares for you, will forgive you, will strengthen you, will give you new life, and for you, that becomes Good News. It is Gospel. Then you consider your own life story — where you have come from, where you are going, what you want to do with your life, to make of your life. And the two stories — your story and God's story — begin to come together, then to intersect, then to combine, so that your story becomes the story of God in your life, and God's history becomes in part the story you live out of God's love and purposes. St. Paul wrote of "Christ in you" [your life and the life of Christ intertwined] — "Christ in you, the hope of glory" (Colossians 1:27).

So we listen to our parents, we listen to our preachers, we listen to the Bible, we listen to the church, we read good books, but instead of getting a set of slogans, a set of ironclad rules, a set of demands, a narrow, negative, angry set of dogmas to defend, we get a LIFE. We walk with God, inspired and guided by the story of God's coming in Jesus Christ, connecting that story with our own so that we, too, live a life of purpose and discipline and care for others. In this we are one with persons in all faiths who teach goodness and not hate.

I was writing the first draft of this message on a September 11, on the first anniversary of 9-1-1 — writing it literally on that day, in the afternoon, in the minister's study of Country Club Christian Church. And my mind kept musing on two events, two, with which I conclude this sermon.

The first involved Todd Beamer, graduate of a Christian school, Wheaton College, where my brother-in-law Paul once taught Old Testament; Todd a young businessman thirty-two years of age, with a beautiful and very pregnant wife Lisa and two children — David and Drew — waiting for him at home; Todd who by cell phone asks a GTE operator to recite with him the Lord's Prayer, and then she hears him say, "C'mon guys, let's roll" — the very words he would use to focus small sons David and Drew on a project — and with other passengers and crew he attacks the terrorists on United Flight 093 and crashes that Boeing 757 into a bare Pennsylvania field instead of the White House or U.S. Capitol on Pennsylvania Avenue.

Todd Beamer could do this because of his theology, his beliefs, born of a relationship with his God, that gave him the courage and faith to risk his life, even to sacrifice his life, to give up wife and children and future, so he could save others. His story had come together with the story of God in Christ Jesus, who also died as a gift of life to others; the two had become one story; and God worked through Todd Beamer, was seen in Todd Beamer, is still seen in Todd Beamer.

The second involved a young man in his office on a top floor of the south tower of the World Trade Center — I never learned his name — who was following directions to get out fast after the north tower was hit and who had descended as far as the 44th floor when, eighteen minutes later, his own building was struck. The impact knocked him to his knees, there was smoke and complete darkness in the stairwell, and in the confusion he was disoriented and terrified, found that he was not moving at all but simply holding on to a blank wall in the blackness. Then, he felt a hand on his shoulder. It was the hand of a brave New York policeman who had come into the building as a rescuer and who was saying to him, "Follow me. I know the way out."

Our Lord says, "For whosoever will save his life shall lose it: but whosoever will lose his life for my sake, the same shall save [find] it" (Luke 9:24).

Our Lord says, "Follow me. I know the way out."

This can be our theology.
This can be our story.
This can be our life.

In the name of our Lord Jesus Christ,

Amen.

Pastoral Prayer

Lord, we believe.
Help thou our unbelief.

We so often want answers, explanations, solutions, conclusions,
    knowing that they seldom come.
But mostly we want to know you, to feel your presence in our lives, to
    be assured of your support and strength, your love and forgiveness.
Help thou our unbelief.

We are selfish. Help us break out of ourselves to care for others.
We pray for those who are sick; help us help them.
We pray for those who are grieving; help us to offer comfort.
We pray for those who are hungry; help us to offer food out of our
    abundance.

We pray for justice in our world; help us to act justly and fairly in our
    home, in our work, in our neighborhood.

O Lord, Give us generosity of spirit. Help thou our unbelief.
O Lord, Give us nobility of vision. Help thou our unbelief.
O Lord, Give us resolve to serve. Help thou our unbelief.
O Lord, Give us the will to care. Help thou our unbelief.

O Lord, Give us the comfort, the friendship, the love we so earnestly
need.
Help thou our unbelief.

Lord, we do believe,

Amen

About the Author

"He ain't never been meant for nothin' but preachin,'" said Clyde Hinshaw, who owned a feed store in Columbia, MO. He was a friend of my father, they served together on some civic boards, and for some reason he took an interest in me during my stumblings through junior high and high school. He said this in a meeting at a kind of crossroads deciding whether I should and could go on to seminary.

Apparently Clyde was right about the preachin'. As I describe in the Preface to this book, I did not go into the pastorate, save for three student pulpits in Missouri and Mississippi. But throughout my whole working life I found myself "called out" to preach, a call to which I always gratefully responded.

These sermons are, I think, a mature expression of that call—at least about as mature as I could get it. They were prepared and preached just before we went to England to lead Harlaxton College, a parallel to earlier work as president of William Jewell College. The near-twelve years at Harlaxton were my last work assignment before retirement. So these messages, as I have reworked them and offer them to you, are a kind of testament, the best I can give you from a long lifetime of trying to understand and live God's truth.

As to the requisite biography, here it is in short: I hold four doctorates, earned and honorary; I have written five previous books plus some 100 articles and reviews; I had a very active speaking career, which was gratifying to me and I hope did some good for others, in both church and civic settings; I served a whole bunch of educational and religious and civic boards, in America and Britain; I was very pleased (and surprised) when an Exxon-funded study included me among the top 5% of America's "most effective collegiate leaders"; and I subsequently held a Visiting Fellowship at Cambridge University in England.

"And all that plus a fiver," I used to say, "might get me a Coffee Grande with hot milk and a blueberry muffin at Starbucks.

My wife Suzanne and I, she a former Collegiate Vice President of William Jewell College, now live in retirement on Turtle Creek in Beloit, Wisconsin. It snows here. Beautifully.

www.ingramcontent.com/pod-product-compliance
Lightning Source LLC
Chambersburg PA
CBHW060445040426
42331CB00044B/2624